Mareile Kaufmann

Ethnic Profiling and Counter-Terrorism

Hamburger Studien zur Kriminologie und Kriminalpolitik

Band 46

LIT

Mareile Kaufmann

Ethnic Profiling and Counter-Terrorism

Examples of European Practice and Possible Repercussions

LIT

Bibliographic information published by the Deutsche Nationalbibliothek
The Deutsche Nationalbibliothek lists this publication in the Deutsche Nationalbibliografie; detailed bibliographic data are available in the Internet at http://dnb.d-nb.de.

ISBN 978-3-643-10447-2

A catalogue record for this book is available from the British Library

Fresnostr. 2 D-48159 Münster
Tel. +49 (0) 2 51-620 320 Fax +49 (0) 2 51-922 60 99
e-Mail: lit@lit-verlag.de http://www.lit-verlag.de

Distribution:

In Germany: LIT Verlag Fresnostr. 2, D-48159 Münster
Tel. +49 (0) 2 51-620 32 22, Fax +49 (0) 2 51-922 60 99, e-Mail: vertrieb@lit-verlag.de

In Austria: Medienlogistik Pichler-ÖBZ GmbH & Co KG
IZ-NÖ, Süd, Straße 1, Objekt 34, A-2355 Wiener Neudorf
Tel. +43 (0) 22 36-63 53 52 90, Fax +43 (0) 22 36-63 53 52 43, e-Mail: mlo@medien-logistik.at

In Switzerland: B + M Buch- und Medienvertriebs AG
Hochstr. 357, CH-8200 Schaffhausen
Tel. +41 (0) 52-643 54 30, Fax +41 (0) 52-643 54 35, e-Mail: order@buch-medien.ch

In the UK by: Global Book Marketing, 99B Wallis Rd, London, E9 5LN
Phone: +44 (0) 20 8533 5800 – Fax: +44 (0) 1600 775 663
http://www.centralbooks.co.uk/html

In North America by:

Transaction Publishers
New Brunswick (U.S.A.) and London (U.K.)

Transaction Publishers
Rutgers University
35 Berrue Circle
Piscataway, NJ 08854

Phone: +1 (732) 445 - 2280
Fax: + 1 (732) 445 - 3138
for orders (U. S. only):
toll free (888) 999 - 6778
e-mail: orders@transactionpub.com

ACKNOWLEDGEMENTS

I would like to thank some very important people.

Prof. Dr. Sebastian Scheerer and Prof. PhD Susanne Krasmann for inspiration and consultancy, as well as the idea and first steps to publish this work.

Åsmund Matzow for artwork and graphic design, for thorough proofreading, for listening to my ideas and for being very supportive throughout the whole process of writing this book.

Irmgard Braselmann and Christoph Hanser for proofreading my work quickly and giving me precious little lectures, for example on data mining.

The Lieselotte-Pongratz-Stiftung, especially Prof. Dr. Timm Kunstreich and Prof. Dr. Michael Lindenberg, who decided to financially support the publication.

My family and friends, who gave me encouragement, inspiration and backup.

"The reliance on actuarial methods actually ends up shaping the social world by accentuating and aggravating the correlations between group traits and criminality."

(Harcourt 2007 : 36)

CONTENTS

Ethnic profiling and Counter-Terrorism 8

Ethnic Profiling in der Terrorismusbekämpfung 9

1. Ethnic Profiling in European Counter-Terrorism – Introducing a Dispute 10

2. Ethnic Profiling and the Actuarial 12

2.1 Actuarial Methods in the Criminal Justice System 12

2.2 Defining the Different Kinds of Profiling 16

3. Possible Work Fields and Methods 18

3.1 Stop and Frisk 18

3.2 Mass Identity Checks 21

3.3 Raids 23

3.4 Arrests and Imprisonment 26

3.5 Vetting Air Passengers 27

3.6 Further Possible Scenarios of Ethnic Profiling and Modern Security Technology 31

4. Possible Implications of Ethnic Profiling 38

4.1 The Deterring Effects of Ethnic Profiling 39

4.2 The Concept of Ethnic Profiling and its Methodological Weaknesses 50

4.3 The Social Aftermath of Ethnic Profiling and Repercussions on Security Policy 73

5. Ethnic Profiling in European Counter-Terrorism – Legal Considerations 87

5.1 European Counter-Terrorism 87

5.2 European Legal Standards Concerning Ethnic Profiling 91

5.3 Weighing the Arguments: the Principle of Proportionality 95

6. Drawing Conclusions 102

References 109

ETHNIC PROFILING AND COUNTER-TERRORISM

Discussion on the controversial practice of ethnic profiling is generally considered an U.S. issue. However, such profiling methods – including their different problematic aspects, are already part of European counter-terrorism strategies. The practice of "Stop and Search", mass identity checks, raids and the vetting of air passengers are just a few examples.

This thesis disputes the effectiveness of such methods with regard to the requested primary effects, the implicit offender's profile and the risks of over- and under-inclusion. Additionally, it considers further secondary effects of this actuarial phenomenon, such as substitution.

Another important aspect that is dealt with is the impact that ethnic profiling in counter-terrorism has on individual rights and freedoms. It impinges on the right to non-discrimination (e.g. Art. 3, para. 3 of the German Constitution) as well as it goes against the interdiction of arbitrary arrest (Art. 9, Universal Declaration of Human Rights) and the principle of proportionality. In this context the dynamic self-enforcing ratchet-effect is of great importance, which again might lead to the emergence of counter-productive reactance and defiant reactions.

Finally, intelligence-led profiling and randomized searches are discussed as feasible alternatives to ethnic profiling in counter-terrorism.

ETHNIC PROFILING IN DER TERRORISMUSBEKÄMPFUNG

Das in den USA kontrovers diskutierte *ethnic profiling* wurde lange Zeit als US-amerikanisches Spezialproblem angesehen. Die unter vielerlei Gesichtspunkten problematischen Profiling-Methoden sind jedoch längst in der europäischen Terrorismusbekämpfung angekommen – so zum Beispiel bei groß angelegten Ausweiskontrollen und Durchsuchungen (Stop and Search), bei Razzien und bei der Erhebung und Weitergabe der Daten von Flugpassagieren.

Die vorliegende Studie problematisiert die Effektivität dieser Methoden im Hinblick auf die angestrebten Primäreffekte, auf das implizite Täterbild und die Risiken von sowohl Über- als auch von Unter-Inklusionen. Darüber hinaus thematisiert die Arbeit weitere naheliegende Sekundär-, bzw. Substitutionseffekte dieses aktuarischen Phänomens.

Problematisch erscheint das *ethnic profiling* im Rahmen der Terrorismusbekämpfung aber auch menschenrechtspolitisch im Hinblick auf Verletzungen des generellen Diskriminierungsverbots (in Deutschland: Art. 3 Absatz 3 des Grundgesetzes), des Schutzes vor willkürlicher Verhaftung (Art. 9 ICCPR) und des Verhältnismäßigkeitsprinzips. In diesem Zusammenhang ist vor allem der sich dynamisch selbst verstärkende *ratchet effect* von Bedeutung, der wiederum zur Reaktanzbildung und damit zu kontraproduktiven Folgen von *ethnic profiling* führen kann.

Abschließend werden unter den Stichworten *intelligence-led profiling* und randomisierte Kontrollen praktikable Alternativen zum *ethnic profiling* in der Terrorismusbekämpfung zur Diskussion gestellt.

1. ETHNIC PROFILING IN EUROPEAN COUNTER-TERRORISM – INTRODUCING A DISPUTE

Since 9/11, research into concepts such as ethnic violence or ethnic terrorism increases steadily, in Europe as well as in the US. Based on the assumption that ethnic or religious terrorism does exist, it seems both necessary and appropriate to develop actuarial methods, such as terrorist profiles, which include information on ethnicity. The implementation of what opponents call 'ethnic profiling'[1] is very controversial, however. Proponents argue that it is logical, as well as more effective, to include ethnicity as a characteristic in profiling. Adversaries enumerate several disadvantages, their main concern being that ethnic profiling intrudes on the right to non-discrimination.

The call for scientific discussion on ethnic profiling in counter-terrorism has been made in recent years, for example by politicians (e.g. Baroness Sarah Ludford MEP), and non-governmental pressure groups (e.g. the Open Society Initiative or Statewatch). Accordingly the subject is very topical and further discussion is needed to ensure that the debate on ethnic profiling has a scientific foundation.

Consequently, this thesis analyzes possible implications of ethnic profiling in counter-terrorism and potential repercussions on security policy, which have not been very prominent in the political discussion on ethnic profiling yet. This thesis does not evaluate the effectiveness of ethnic profiling empirically, however. Primary and secondary effects will be discussed on a theoretical basis. For this reason speculative elements may occur in the course of the argumentation, but a considerable amount of the thesis will be devoted to giving examples from the European counter-terrorism context[2]

[1] The use of the term 'ethnic profiling' in this thesis should not be construed as an indication of the researcher's position. Here, it refers to the process of implying 'ethnicity' as a characteristic in (predictive) profiling and will be used as a standard-term to simplify matters. Some authors use the term 'racial profiling' instead. The meaning of both terms is the same.

[2] Some examples might be taken from the US or the Israeli-Palestinian conflict, though, but only as a means of demonstrating possible outcomes of a conflict that is more advanced than the situation in Europe and that also involved ethnic profiling.

taken from articles, reports[3] and scientific studies, to typify the arguments and expose forms of appearance of ethnic profiling.

This thesis commences with a short introduction of actuarial methods in the criminal justice context and definitions of different kinds of profiling. The subsequent chapter summarizes possible work fields and methods involving ethnic profiling in European counter-terrorism. This also includes examples of modern surveillance-technology, such as data mining. Examples of further work fields include 'Stop and Search' or raids conducted by the police on the basis of ethnicity.

The main part focuses on possible implications of ethnic profiling. It starts with the demonstration of the deterring effects of ethnic profiling. These are classified as primary effects: for a short while ethnic profiling leads to fewer terrorist attacks. Subsequently, methodological weaknesses of the concept of ethnic profiling will be pointed out. In the following discussion a possible model of the social aftermath of ethnic profiling and its repercussions on security policy is developed. These occurrences are classified as secondary effects: methodological breaches, such as over- and under-inclusion and substitution lead to the alienation of the targeted minority group. This, again, entails strain and possibly more attacks.

The following chapter is devoted to legal considerations, including European legal standards, for example on non-discrimination, which can be consulted while discussing the deployment of ethnic profiling in counter-terrorism. These considerations eventually lead to a proportionality test on ethnic profiling. This proportionality test summarizes and weighs all the preceding arguments and systematically leads to the result of this thesis, namely that ethnic profiling in counter-terrorism is likely to produce considerable negative repercussions on security policy. Consequently, the concluding chapter introduces alternatives to ethnic profiling in counter-terrorism, such as intelligence-led profiling. It gives an overview of future prospects and how negative implications can be avoided, for example by using clear legal frameworks.

---

[3] Some examples will be taken from Internet-portals, which cannot be considered as scientific sources. However, they are included to give examples, which may help to clarify the subjective impact ethnic profiling can have on Muslim communities.

2. ETHNIC PROFILING AND THE ACTUARIAL

2.1 Actuarial Methods in the Criminal Justice System

> "In this day and age, making parole decisions without benefit of a good, research-based risk assessment instrument clearly falls short of accepted best practice." (APAI 2003 : 35)

An Increasing Trend

Since the last two decades of the twentieth century there has been an increasing trend toward using risk-assessment instruments, algorithms and profiling in the criminal justice system. Selective incapacitation, parole prediction, predictions of future dangerousness, and three-strikes laws are just a few examples of these actuarial procedures (Harcourt 2007 : 16ff). All of the actuarial methods rely on "(…) the mechanical combining of information for classification purposes, and the resultant probability figure which is an empirically determined relative frequency" (Meel 1954 : 3). However, most of the criminal justice decision-making involves probabilistic reasoning and there is almost no possibility of avoiding it. Actuarial methods in a narrower sense though, "(…) do not rest simply on probabilities but on statistical correlations between group traits and group criminal offending rates" (Harcourt 2007 : 18).

The general mechanisms of actuarial methods in criminal justice, and more specifically in policing, are deterrence and efficiency. Both are combined in the utilitarian model of rational action: the deterrent effect on the offender increases proportionally with the 'cost' factor, in this case the higher probability of being detected and punished. Considering the costs and benefits of the planned crime, the offender refrains from his plan. This process is called elasticity and results in a decrease of crime. At the same time the efficiency of the police detecting crimes committed by the targeted group rises. To phrase this presupposition as a policing strategy: the police target a certain group of offenders until the offending rate falls – at best to the same level as that of the general population. The underlying assumption by the law enforcement personnel is that different target groups react similarly to policing and that elasticity reduces the targeted group's offending rate (Ibid. : 23).

The Rise of Actuarial Methods in the Criminal Justice Context

The quality of contemporary actuarial methods is most likely a result of prediction instruments developed in the first half of the 1920s. Different methods, such as setting out group-factors and group-trait offending rates, were first approaches to parole prediction[1], modeled on findings of "(…) the same scientific procedure employed by insurance companies when they estimate the probable cost of insuring new applicants on the basis of their experience with the past death rates of insured persons of similar characteristics" (Hart 1923 : 411). These approaches to parole prediction were a counterpart to clinical approaches, involving the medical expertise of a specialist.

These ideas originated from a turn towards the individualization of punishment. Instead of ignoring the variety of cases, the increased knowledge about identifiable causes of crime, such as the "(…) correlations between criminality and home conditions, physical traits, genetic makeup, and neighborhood environment" (Harcourt 2007 : 44f), changed the decisive elements of predictability and, therefore, sentencing. Paradoxically this turn to particular law enforcement, again, fueled the actuarial: what started with the identification of group factors to predict individual success or failure of parole later developed into an elaborate questionnaire used for offender interviewing. Today, one of the most popular prediction instruments is called Level of Services Inventory-Revised (v. i.), which was developed in the 1970s. It asks for several risk factors concerning the offender's criminal history, education/employment, finances, family/marital status, accommodations, leisure/recreation, companions, alcohol /drug problems, emotional/personal issues and attitude/ orientation (Ibid. : 78ff).

---

[1] These methodological achievements can be traced back to scientists such as the Chicago School Sociologists E.W. Burgess 'method of parole prediction'; Ferris F. Laune's 'prognasio', he was a PhD at the Illinois State Penitentiary; Sam B. Warner, who was the director of the Committee on Criminal Records at the Institute of Criminal Law and Criminology in Eugene, Oregon and identified group factors that helped in parole prediction or Hornell Hart, a former researcher at the Iowa Child welfare Research Station, who developed an actual prediction instrument (Harcourt 2007 : 39). In the latter half of the twentieth century the turn from the welfare to the correctional state revived another scientific debate about risk-assessment, punishment and social control, influenced by sociologists of punishment such as Katherine Beckett, Stanley Cohen and David Garland.

I. Criminal History
1. Any prior convictions?
2. Two or more prior convictions?
3. Three or more convictions?
4. Three or more present offenses?
5. Arrested under age 16?
6. Ever incarcerated upon conviction?
7. Escape history from a correctional facility?
8. Ever punished for institutional misconduct?
9. Change made for probation/parole suspended during prior community supervision?
10. Official record of assault/violence?

II. Education/Employment
11. Currently employed?
12. Frequently unemployed?
13. Never employed for a full year?
14. Ever fired?
15. Less than regular grade 10?
16. Less than regular grade 12?
17. Suspended or expelled at least once?
18. Participation /performance
19. Peer interactions
20. Authority interactions

III. Financial
21. Problems?
22. Reliance upon social assistance?

IV. Family/Marital
23. Dissatisfaction with marital partner or equivalent?
24. Non-rewarding, parental
25. Non-rewarding, other relative
26. Criminal family/spouse?

V. Accommodations
27. Unsatisfactory
28. Three or more address changes last year?
29. High-crime neighborhood?

VI. Leisure/Recreation
30. Absence of recent participation in an org. activity?
31. Could make better use of time.

VII. Companions
32. A social isolate?
33. Some criminal acquaintances?
34. Some criminal friends?
35. Few anti-criminal acquaintances?
36. Few anti-criminal friends?

VII. Alcohol/Drug Problem
37. Alcohol problem, ever?
38. Drug problem, ever?
39. Alcohol problem, currently?
40. Drug problem, currently?
41. Law violations?
42. Marital/family?
43. School/work?
44. Medical?
45. Other indicators?

IX. Emotional/Personal
46. Moderate interference?
47. Severe interference, active psychosis?
48. Mental health treatment, past?
49. Mental health treatment, present?
50. Psychological assessment indicated?

X. Attitudes/Orientation
51. Supportive of crime.
52. Unfavorable toward convention.
53. Poor, toward sentence?
54. Poor, toward supervision?

Fig. 1: LSI-R Instrument (Harcourt 2007 : 81)

The Genesis of Criminal Profiling

However, there are different actuarial methods in the sentencing and policing context even though their general approach is fairly similar. Profiles are developed to help police officers identify potential offenders. They are based on the assumption that certain character traits correlate with certain offending rates. A more detailed definition will be given in the next chapter.

The first profiles were developed in the late 1960s in response to a series of plane hijackings that required advanced safety arrangements on the ground. The measures involved the screening of flight passengers with a behavioral profile, the content of which would be kept secret. Suspicious passengers would be screened by metal detectors[2] or, in case of emergency, be questioned. These first experiences with profiling were not very successful (Harris 2002 : 17f).

The subsequent serial-killer profile, developed by the FBI, didn't rest solely on behavioral data. It included psychological information from interviews with serial killers that had been caught, such as the modus operandi and the killer's motivation. Apart from the fact that serial-killer profiles had a very low rate of appliance, there was almost no data about the number of cases that ended with arrests due to the use of these profiles. Therefore it was not possible to evaluate its effectiveness (Ibid. : 18f).

However, in the 1980s the Drug Enforcement Administration (DEA) under John Marcello and Paul Markonni composed a pioneering 'drug courier profile' which was applied to a broader range of offences. This was the first profile designed for the proactive detection of offenders and was employed in the DEA's Airport interdiction program (Ibid : 19ff).

> "Before developing the drug courier profile, DEA agents learned the modus operandi of cross-country drug distributors and couriers through conversations with undercover operators, informants, and cooperative defendants – those arrested on drug charges as well as convicted codefendants who turned state's evidence." (Becton 1987 : 426)

Examples of common characteristics of drug couriers could be: (1) the buying of tickets with large amounts of cash; (2) traveling under a different name; (3) traveling to suspicious so-called 'drug-source cities'; (4) staying at a destination only for a few hours; (5) appearing nervous; (6) not

---

[2] Today's metal detectors and x-ray detectors used for every passenger on almost every airport worldwide are a follow-up version of these so-called magnetometers (Harris 2002 : 18).

checking in any luggage (Harris 2002 : 20). However, the profile was considered as a 'collective experience' rather than a national profile, because "(…) each airport unit has developed its own set of drug courier characteristics on the basis of that unit's experience (…) Furthermore, the profile is not rigid, but is constantly modified in light of experience" (Becton 1987 : 433). Similarly informal was the 'birth' of profiling on the highway, when DEA agent Bob Vogel found 'cumulative similarities' of drug couriers on the Interstate 95 in the early 1980s (Harris 2002 : 21ff).

According to these examples of different styles of profiling, it is important to distinguish between formal profiles and less structured informally collected data, which is not systematically analyzed. In spite of all that, informal profiling might be more present in contemporary policing than formal profiling (Harris 2002 : 21ff). To understand the concept of profiling as it is used in this thesis, the next chapter gives an overview of the different definitions.

2.2 Defining the Different Kinds of Profiling

Criminal Profiling

Since police personnel and procedures are limited, law enforcement is inevitably selective. The creation and analysis of perpetrators' profiles are methods designed to simplify and optimize criminal prosecution. That way criminal profiling can be considered as the systematic association of physical, psychological and behavioral traits with particular offenses or groups of offenses and their use as a basis for making investigative decisions (Harris 2002 : 11ff).

Using gathered evidence of a certain criminal act to identify the offender of that particular crime, is known as descriptive profiling. This kind of ex post-profiling may contain information on the perpetrator, such as age, appearance or profession. It can be used to prevent the suspect, e.g. a serial killer, from committing further crime.

Predictive profiles however, are designed to find perpetrators ex ante, perpetrators that may be responsible for or participating in future crime as yet unknown to the police. Accordingly, it is used against a much broader category of crime (Harris 2002 : 16ff). To date there are very few statistics on how effective predictive profiling really is, although the quality of profiling depends to a certain extent on statistical evidence: "(…) factors that are statistically proven to correlate with certain criminal conduct can be effective law enforcement tools" (Moeckli 2006 : 6).

Thus, profiles are arrayed along the time-dimension – ex post or ex ante. In addition to that, profiles may also vary with the kind of data upon which they are based. Descriptive profiles derive from external and observable characteristics, that is physical data, which is taken from criminal records. Other profiles contain behavioral or psychological information, such as clinical reports or details on social life. Some profiles mix both kinds of data (Harcourt 2007 : 104).

Ethnic and Racial Profiling

Successful descriptive profiling obligates police officers to use skin color or race as a criterion for the appearance of a suspect, provided the police have this information. However, if predictive profiles contain variables such as race, religion or skin color, ethnic profiling (q.v. racial profiling) is generated. It acts on the assumption that implicating ethnicity in a criminal profile increases the chances of effective law enforcement. The proponents of ethnic profiling argue that "(t)he disproportionately large number of minorities reflected in arrest and incarceration statistics is further proof (…) that skin color is a valid indicator of a greater propensity to commit crime" (Harris 2002 : 11).

Whereas the European Union Agency for Fundamental Rights (FRA) defines ethnic profiling as

> "(…) actions initiated by agents/officials of the State (...) that treat people differently solely on the basis of their real or assumed 'race', ethnicity, religion or national origin, rather than responding to the behaviour of an individual, a suspect description or other intelligence" (FRA – Ethnic Profiling Project 2007 : 2).

It is important to distinguish between ethnic profiling and ethnic monitoring, though. The latter is conducted with the individual's permission and according to data protection laws that allow the gathering of sensitive information for statistical reasons "(…) with the purpose of using this information to highlight discriminatory practices; for example, discriminatory practices in employment, education, housing and by agents/officials of the State" (Ibid. : 2).

3. POSSIBLE WORK FIELDS AND METHODS

Involving Ethnic Profiling in European Counter-Terrorism

Criminal profiling comes into play when supposed suspects are checked or kept under surveillance. There are different police actions that may involve ethnicity as a criterion to monitor someone.

3.1 Stop and Frisk

One monitoring method that might implement ethnic profiling is the so-called 'Stop and Frisk' (q.v. 'Stop and Search').

> "A stop is a detention of a person by the police. It differs from a seizure or an arrest in that it is presumed to be temporary. A frisk is a search, but like a stop it is a limited type of police action that (…) can include only a 'pat down' on the suspect's outer clothing. No further search – nor reaching into a pocket or under a shirt – can take place[1]." (Harris 2002 : 37)

As a general rule, there has to be evidence of a real threat to conduct a frisk. However, some categories of crime are in part jurisdictionally considered dangerous and lead to an automatic frisk, such as burglary, gambling and drug dealing, or loitering in a 'high-crime area' (Ibid. : 41ff).

Stop and Frisk on the Street – The Example of the UK Terrorism Act

In 2000 the United Kingdom introduced the Terrorism Act. Section 44 authorizes police in uniform to stop and search (1) vehicles and passengers of the vehicles and (2) pedestrians and anything carried by them in authorized areas. However it says under (3) that "An authorization under subsection (1) or (2) may be given only if the person giving it considers it expedient for the prevention of acts of terrorism" (Terrorism Act 2000: Section 44). Official British police guidelines indicate that exceptionally

---

[1] Nevertheless, a frisk can be very thorough, because "(...) the officer must feel with sensitive fingers every portion of the suspect's body. A thorough search must be made of the suspect's arms and armpits, waistline and back, the groin and area about the testicles, and the entire surface of the legs down to the feet" (Priar/Martin 1954 : 481).

> "(…) it is appropriate for officers to take account of a person's ethnic origin in selecting persons to be stopped in response to a specific terrorist threat (for example, some international terrorist groups are associated with particular ethnic identities)." (Police and Criminal Evidence Act: Code A, 2.25)

After the July 7th attacks, which were carried out by Britons of Pakistani descent, areas surrounding the transport infrastructure and big urban areas were classified as areas that can be searched with no reasonable cause. Since then, people of Asian descent have been five times more likely to be stopped and searched than white people:

> "Unpublished figures from July 7 to August 10 showed that the transport police carried out 6,747 stops under anti-terrorism laws, with the majority in London. The force recorded 2,390 stops of Asian people, 35% of the total, and 2,168 of white people, who were 32% of the total. In London Asian people comprise 12% of the population, while white people are 63%. In June the force stopped 408 people nationwide, with less of a focus on Asian people than a month later. Of that month's stops, 51% were white, 8.6% were African-Caribbean, and 16.2% were Asian." (Dodd 2005 : 1)

Yet before the London bombings of 2005, the Muslim Council of Britain claimed that statistics of 2001/2 and 2002/3 document an increase of the number of South Asians who were stopped and searched by the police of 302% in 2002/3, and less than 1% of the people stopped under sections 44 (1) and (2) were arrested (MCB 2004 : 1).

These instances were not denied, neither by the police, nor by the UK minister responsible for counter-terrorism, who mentioned before the Commons Home Affairs Committee in March 2005 that some counter-terrorism powers would be disproportionately experienced by the Muslim community (Dodd/Travis 2005 : 1). Whereas the Minister later retracted the statement, the transport police's chief constable Ian Johnston said in August 2005: "Intelligence-led stop and searches have got to be the way (…) We should not waste time searching old white ladies. It is going to be disproportionate. It is going to be young men, not exclusively, but it may be disproportionate when it comes to ethnic groups" (Dodd 2005 : 1). Furthermore, the Metropolitan Police Authority report conceded that Stop and Search rates have become an indicator for racial profiling in London (MCB 2004 : 1). Mr. Clarke, Deputy Assistant Commissioner of the Metropolitan Police, considered the Section 44 Stop and Searches as having been implemented in a way that caused difficulties and was warning that these kind of anti-terror measures would alienate the Muslim community (Travis 2006a : 1)[2].

The Muslim Community, however, questioned whether the Stop and Search practice was intelligence-led and mentioned that this practice was disproportionate at an unacceptable scale (Dodd 2005 : 2). The Muslim Association of Britain stated that such a policy would not help " (…) in terms of building a relationship or trust between the communities" (Kirby 2005 : 1). On the other hand, the Chief Superintendent of the National Black Police Association, Ali Dizaei, said that he agreed ethnic profiling was acceptable provided searches were carried out politely and with respect (Ibid. : 1). Marian Fitzgerald, a criminologist of the University of Kent, pointed at the long-term consequences and questioned the effectiveness of such a tool in tackling a terrorist suspect (Dodd 2005 : 1f). The wide discretionary powers of the police and the absence of juridical review, in this case the monitoring of the police, creates a disequilibrium: on the one hand the police may develop a sense of impunity and the targeted community might feel powerless and a feeling of resentment might arouse (OSI 2007 : 3).

Consulting the Stop and Search Figures of the London Police of 2007, the numbers of general Stops and Searches, as well as the number of Asians being in a Stop and Search under Terrorism Act dropped notably in comparison to 2005, although a slight ethnic disproportion is still noticeable. While the general population consists of 85% Whites, 7% Asians and 3% Blacks, the ratio of people stopped and searched is 59% Whites, 12% Asians and 14% Blacks. For Stop and Search under Terorism Act, the ratio is 66% Whites, 13% Asians and 9% Blacks (City of London Police 2007 : 1). The homepage of the Metropolitan Police Service provides helpful information about Stop and Search. The website contains details about e.g. the reason of a stop or about adequate behavior whilst stopped. This initiative by the

[2] So does the Muslim Community mention: "Just as an entire generation of young black men were alienated through Stop and Search practice, we are deeply worried that the same could now be occurring again, this time to young Muslim men." (MCB 2004 : 1)

police can be considered as an advance towards cooperation with the citizens (Metropolitan Police 2008 : 1ff.).

3.2 Mass Identity Checks

Another large-scale version of the phenomenon described above is performed in mass identity document checks. These checks are designed to single out those that are presumably involved in terrorism. Most of the checks are carried out at 'sensitive sites', such as metros, train stations, or commercial centers. In some cases this kind of police action is very likely to be based on ethnic profiling, for instance when law enforcement officers deliberately carry out mass identity checks at sites where officials believe there to be a high concentration of Muslims: telephone calling centers, halal restaurants, mosques, and specific neighborhoods. The operations can take several hours (OSI 2007 : 6f). Interviews with law enforcement officials suggested that most of the checks are wide-ranging information-gathering exercises and not based on concrete intelligence (Goldston 2006 : 4). Cases of mass identity checks involving ethnic profiling were reported to happen in France, Italy and Germany.

Between 25 and 30 mosques have been targeted for mass identity checks in Germany, mostly connected to Friday Prayers. Individuals with no valid ID have been taken to police stations and held for several hours until their status was verified (Ibid. : 4)[3]. Excerpts taken from Islamic German portals give examples:

> "Am Freitag, den 13.12.02 fanden sich in der Al-Famq Omar Moschee ca. 200 Gläubige zum Freitagsgebet ein. Während des

[3] 'Aktion Courage' even documents cases of police power against foreign looking people, who are more often target of checks without a given suspicion – and yet sometimes victims of abuse: "Polizeigewalt sei keine gewöhnliche Gewalt, sondern sie wird als Gewalt des Staates wahrgenommen. (...) Hinter den 70 Beispielen verbergen sich Gewaltfolgen für 110 Menschen; nicht immer waren es einzelne Opfer, die die Schläge und Tritte genervter oder übereifriger und vermutlich rassistisch gesinnter Polizisten erlitten." (Islam.de 2004 : 1f) Rough translation: "Police power is no ordinary power, but is perceived as state power. There are 70 examples, which led to consequences of violence against 110 people; it weren't always singular victims, who were kicked and beaten by nerved, overeager or racist police officers."

> Gebetes stürmte eine Einsatztruppe der Polizei in Kampfuniform und mit Schlagstöcken bewaffnet die Moschee und besetzten den Gebetsraum." [4] (Adel 2002 : 1)

A similar scenario was described on a different portal:

> "Innerhalb weniger Monate wurden die Muslime in Braunschweig nun zum dritten Mal nach dem Freitagsgebet in ihrer Religionsausübung gestört. Es traf diesmal erneut den Gebetsraum des 'Deutschsprachigen Muslimkreises in Braunschweig e.V.'"[5] (IGMG 2004 : 1)[6].

Later it says:

> "Zwischen 12 und 14 Uhr haben sich am Freitag während des Freitagsgebets uniformierte und zivile Beamte der Polizei Osnabrück an den Ein- und Ausgängen der Osnabrücker Moscheegemeinde der IGMG positioniert und alle Moscheebesucher einer Ausweiskontrolle unterzogen. Die Maßnahmen wurden im Rahmen der "verdachtsunabhängigen Kontrollen" durchgeführt, mit denen nun seit 2004 Muslime immer wieder während des Freitagsgebetes belästigt werden, ohne dass auch nur der geringste Verdacht gegenüber der Moscheegemeinde oder ihren Besuchern bestehen würde."[7] (IGMG 2005 : 1)

---

[4] (Rough translation) "On Friday, the 13th of December 2002, approximately 200 believers gathered for friday prayers. During the prayers police force in fighting uniform and with clubs stormed and occupied the prayer room."

[5] (Rough translation) "Only within a few months Muslims in Braunschweig were again disrupted while practicing religion. Again it affected the prayer room of the "Deutschsprachigen Muslimkreises in Braunschweig e.V."

[6] It is important to mention that the IGMG is used as a source of information, like any of the other cited newspaper articles. The authenticity of any of these sources cannot be proven, but they function as a reference to the objective or subjective impression of Muslims being treated disproportionately in anti-terrorism strikes. In the German Constitution the IGMG is considered as a group with a fundamental ideology ('legalistischer Islmasimus'). However, some parties question the classification of this group (Schiffauer 2006 : 239ff).

[7] (Rough translation) "On Friday between noon and two pm, during the Friday prayers, police officers sited and occupied the entrances and exits of the IGMG mosque in Osnabrück and stopped and searched all the visitors of the mosque. The "checks without a given suspicion", which are continuously torment

Security officials suggested that there was little expectation that the police would be lucky enough to detect a terrorist by means of identity checks. However, mass identity document controls serve different functions. They may seek a demonstration effect, to make counter-terrorism efforts visible, but beyond that there are collateral benefits, primarily in immigration enforcement outcomes of identity checks (OSI 2007 : 17).

In addition to that, there is a system dedicated to monitoring all visa applicants to an EU member state called Visa Information System (VIS), which was implemented in the response to the 9/11 attacks. It holds personal information, such as nationality at birth, grounds for refusal, and links to other applications. As a central database that links all border checkpoints, it is designed to manage biometric data (Article 29 Working Party 2005 : 11f). In the wake of the London bombings the UK presidency of the EU has been calling for a broadening of the access privileges to VIS, to permit all EU law enforcement agencies to access all data held there (Privacy International 2005 : 4).

3.3 Raids

A raid may be based on specific probative information leading officials to suspect a particular individual of supporting or promoting severe criminal activities. However, in counter-terrorism efforts, law enforcement officials conduct preventive raids in a manner that frequently appear focused on Muslim faith rather than on concrete evidence (OSI 2007 : 9). International human rights organizations report that

> "(…) since September 11, thousands of Muslims have been subjected to screening of their personal data, house searches, interrogations, and arrests solely because their profiles have matched certain base criteria, foremost of which is an affiliation with Islam" (IHF 2007 : 78).

Muslim places of worship, business and private homes have been targets for raids and mass searches aimed at disrupting the support base for terrorism. A few of them have led to further investigation and in a limited number of cases, there has been solid evidentiary basis for the action. Since

---

Muslims during the Friday prayers since 2004, are made without any existing suspicion against the IGMG mosque or their visitors."

most of the raids did not produce arrests or charges for terrorist offences, the high level of publicity surrounding many raids reflect a desire to demonstrate the 'toughness on terrorism' (OSI 2007 : 9f). However, some raids have led to arrests, for instance in Perugia in 2007 as the BBC reports:

> "Police in central Italy say they have uncovered a bomb school for Islamist militants after raiding a mosque in Perugia and making three arrests. Evidence of training in explosives and poisons, and instructions on flying a Boeing 747 were reportedly found. Police said the suspected cell had links to a group associated with Osama Bin Laden's al-Queda network. They seized the imam and two other men, all Maroccans, and have a warrant for a fourth man believed to be abroad. (…) The director of the Cultural Institute of the Italian Islamic Community, Sheikh Abdul Adid Palazzi, told the BBC News '(…) Most mosques are controlled by extremist pro-terror organizations – 90% of mosques, (…) And I think the percentage is more or less the same in Italy, Britain, France and Germany.'" (BBC 2007 : 1f)

A similar discovery was made in London, four years before the incident in Perugia:

> "British anti-terror police found a mini-arsenal of weapons when they raided a London mosque linked to a number of key terrorist suspects. Officers found a stun gun, an imitation weapon which fires blanks and a CS gas canister during a search of the North London Central Mosque in Finsbury Park on Monday. A large number of passports, identity cards and credit cards were also found. In all, seven men were arrested and have been questioned under the UK's Terrorism 2000 Act." (CNN 2003 : 1f)

Similar raids and arrests were made in Germany. The confiscated items however, did not hint at a planned terrorist attack:

> "They said that an operation involving more than 800 officers, police had raided 50 addresses across Germany and confiscated faked passports, computer data and militant Islamic propaganda (…) But police said they had found no evidence indicating that the group planned to carry out a terrorist attack. Mr Stern[8] said the objective

[8] Mr. Stern is Germany's former chief state prosecutor.

> of the raids had been to destroy the logical base of the network." (Paterson 2005 : 1)

Another German raid ended with no arrests or confiscations at all:

> "Armed police are searching a mosque in Hamburg after a report that a man was inside preparing explosives for an attack (…) Streets were blocked off but there were no initial reports of anyone being found matching the description given in a tip-off." (BBC 2002 : 1)

In France, raids on mosques are coordinated by 'regional centers to combat radical Islam' (poles régionaux de little contre l'islam radical). The centers were established in each of France's 22 metropolitan regions in 2005 by order of the French Ministry of the Interior. In addition to surveillance activities, they are mandated by the French General Secret Services to use administrative powers to impede and disturb radical Islamists' businesses, which may be fast food restaurants, cafes, call centers, bookstores and security companies.

> "In 2005, in the greater Paris region (Ile de France) alone, 88 raids were carried out involving 1,173 people, 185 of whom were taken into custody and eight prosecuted. Activities increased in 2006, with 93 raids carried out between January 1 and May 15, 2006. (…) Any Muslim owned or Muslim managed businesses that the authorities consider 'radical' can be singled out for raids and controls beyond normal administrative and regulatory checks. The concept of 'radical Islam' is not defined." (OSI 2007 : 10)

The Netherlands however, has a different surveillance-based system in effect to prevent jihadi terrorism. Dutch intelligence services indeed use religion as a basis for monitoring Muslim organizations:

> "Monitoring is conducted on the basis of generalizations about the type of Islam that groups practice, promote or support, rather than specific information about activities in a particular Mosque or organization. The surveillance covers streams of Islam that are held to be dangerous even when non-violent, on the theory that they may be hotbeds of terrorist radicalization." (Ibid.: 13)

3.4 Arrests and Imprisonment

Some European countries have already been practicing the detention of terrorism suspects for a long time. France's preemptive system involves two types of detention: pre-charge detention (garde à vue) and pre-trial detention (détention provisoire). The investigating magistrates (juge d'instruction) can authorize a pre-charge detention up to six days, if the case involves terrorism. Suspects are neither entitled to see their lawyers for 72 hours, nor are they notified of their right to silence. Pre-trial detention can last up to four years. "Such detention is by law recommended only if it is necessary to preserve material evidence, prevent witness pressure, prevent flight, or to protect the accused" (Shapiro 2008 : 3).

Since abuses of pre-trial detention became public, all pre-trial detentions have to be approved by an independent magistrate (juge des libertés et de la détention). Yet, further allegations of torture took place in detention. Therefore, France created an independent authority for the monitoring of all places of detention, which is not yet operational. In addition to the abuses that had happened at pre-trial detentions, this kind detention policy runs the risk of enforcing counter-terrorism in a disproportionate manner:

> "(…) the French counterterrorism apparatus is extraordinarily repressive and intrusive and this repression falls particularly on specific groups, primarily Muslims and Corsicans. During the wave of terrorist attacks in 1995, French authorities detained some 70,000 people for questioning; the vast majority of them were North African." (Ibid. : 3f).

In Britain the pre-charge detention was originally limited to 48 hours. It was extended several times: first, to 14 days and then to 28 days with a high court judge's approval. A new bill is currently before parliament, proposing to extend the detention period to 42 days (Ibid. : 4f). That makes Britain having the longest terrorist detention by far:

> "Liberty staff interviewed terrorism specialists and lawyers in 15 countries. Their research found that in the U.S. the detention limit is two days, in France it is six, Italy four and in Turkey suspects can be held for 7-1/2 days. In Spain, where 191 people died in the 2004 Madrid train bombings, there is a five-day detention limit.

> The closest any country comes to Britain's month-long limit is Australia with 12 days." (Leggatt/Addison 2007 : 1)

After the 1970s the number of detained terrorism suspects was at its highest level between 2001 and 2004: 664 people were detained under the Terrorism Act. 118 were charged under the Act while 135 were charged under other legislation, 315 were released without charge. Already in 2004 Barry Hugill of the human rights campaign 'Liberty' pointed out that people of Muslim descent were unreasonably and disproportionately charged: "When it is compared to the low number of people actually convicted of an offence it creates the sense among the Muslim community that people are being pulled in against whom there is very little real evidence" (O'Neill 2004 : 1).

Likewise people from countries with a majority of Muslim population such as Afghanistan, Morocco and Pakistan, have been arrested by Italian Police. Since 2001 over 200 highly publicized arrests of migrants have been made. Only two have resulted in findings of guilt in terrorist related crimes, most detainees were released without charge. A lot of the arrests reached high media attention, whereas the coverage of the releases was less extensive. This discrepancy leaves the impression to the public that "(…) the British criminal justice system is successfully prosecuting Muslim terrorists, although in reality most of those Muslims who are arrested on terrorism allegations are never charged with any terrorism offence" (OSI 2007 : 12).

3.5 Vetting Air Passengers

There are different kinds of air passenger monitoring. Metal detectors or passport controls are some of them. With the storage of certain passenger information, though, (terrorist) profiling is made possible. Since 2004, for example, there has been an ongoing discussion between the EU and the US about the storage and transmission of air passenger data. As a part of a Europe-wide security net to counter terrorism[9], the US obtained access to 34

---

[9] Besides the Passenger Name Record System (PNR) it encompasses further airport security checks (enhanced hand luggage search), the barring of information material on building bombs on the web, intensified research into explosives and curbing the availability of liquid explosives, the creation of a rapid response force to deal with the aftermath of terrorist attacks and the tackling of radicalization by training imams at European level, as in building a

data sets, such as address, credit card information and dietary requirements of each flight passenger, to identify and select potential terrorists. However, the agreement from Mai 2004 was annulled in Mai 2006 – not because of privacy advocates' criticism, but due to an ineligible legal foundation. An interim agreement with similar content was made in October 2006 (Tomik 2007 : 1ff). By means of a scoring-system, the passenger details could be matched against a series of behavioral patterns for establishing a risk-profile to identify 'high-risk passengers'. These passengers could be detained, questioned and dismissed. However, the purpose specification of the transmitted data remained indistinct for data protection officers.

Recent EU-Plans on Air Passenger Profiling

In November 2007 the EU commission proposed a new scheme for advanced air passenger screening, which would mirror the US Passenger Name Record System (PNR). It stated that from the first half of 2009 airlines traveling to or from the EU would be required to transmit 19 pieces of data on each of their passengers – including name and address, full itinerary, billing data and baggage information (EC Document 0/243/2007: ANNEX I). A combination of operational expertise, specific intelligence and historical analysis would be used to develop a profiling system to assess travelers' terrorist risk, which could result in denied entry. The collected data would be stored for five years and for further eight years in a 'dormant' database. The scheme would not apply to intra-European flights and the proposal excludes the sharing of 'sensitive' data, defined as anything that could reveal a passenger's race or religion, political views or sexual preferences. This kind of data would automatically be filtered out and deleted, in case it was transmitted to the US (Ibid. : Art. 1ff).

EU Commissioner Franco Frattini defended the project saying that "(t)he Union is at least as much a potential target of a terrorist attack as the United States, and the use and analysis of passenger name records is an important law enforcement tool to protect our citizens" (EurActiv 2007 : 1). French Interior Minister Michelle Alliot-Marie agreed: "I am in favour. It is paradoxical that we don't have here what we have with the United States", referring to the 2004 agreement on transmission of flight passenger data to

---

'European Islam' (Travis 2006b : 1).

the US (Melander 2008 : 1f). Spanish Secretary of State for Security Antonio Camacho also backed the plans, referring to the implementation of a similar system (Advanced Passenger Information – API)[10] in 2007: "Since March, we have analyzed millions of (pieces of) data and this has allowed us to have a better idea of who enters our country and to stop (…) almost 400 persons last year" (Ibid. : 2). Yet this was a crucial point of the opponents' criticism: the plan did not suggest what would happen to the data after it was collected. Statewatch editor Tony Bunyan commented: "There is little evidence that the gathering of 'mountain upon mountain' of data on the activity of every person in the EU makes a significant contribution (to tackling terrorism)" (Statewatch 2007 : 2)[11]. The EU data protection work group reached a similar conclusion: the processing of the data would not necessarily support the fight against terrorism (Unwatched 2007 : 2). EU anti-terrorism coordinator Gilles de Kerchove acknowledged that ministers still needed to decide how the scheme would work (Melander 2008 : 1). Furthermore the risk assessment for each passenger acts upon criteria – which are again based on national laws (EC Document 0/243/2007: Art 3.3), so the basis of each risk assessment could differ with every member state's watch-lists and criteria (Statewatch 2007 : 5). The text of the proposal provides a further breach: article 3.5 says that risk assessment should "(…) identify persons who are maybe involved in a terrorist or organized crime offence, as well as their associates" (EC Document 0/243/2007: Art. 3.5). With the phrase 'may be involved' and 'associates' two very vague categories are put together and an unlimited number of 'maybe' – or 'may not be'-involved people can be added to the file (Statewatch 2007 : 5).

Dutch Liberal MEP Sophie in 't Veld suggested a thorough evaluation of the effectiveness of existing passenger data schemes (EurActiv 2007 : 1), such as the European API system that despite an EU regulation was still

---

[10] The 2004 EC Directive on the collection of API due to be put into effect by all Member States by 2006 was merely realized by Spain. The data required by API (held in the machine readable zone of EU passports): Name, nationality, passport number, date of birth; details of the flight: Place of entry in the EU, plane code, departure and arrival time, number of passengers, point of embarkation (Statewatch 2007 : 1).

[11] Furthermore statewatch criticized the length of time that data of passengers who had been cleared as a 'risk' was supposed to be stored (Statewatch 2007 : 7).

not implemented by the majority of the member states. Furthermore only three member states out of 27 – UK, France and Denmark – have enacted legislation for the capture and use of PNR yet (Statewatch 2007 : 3). The Netherlands, Austria, Sweden and Hungary expressed concerns about the proposal (Krempl 2008: 1). That may be due to the high costs of the program or to the fact that the proposal does not refer to the EC directive of 1995, according to which the storage of PNR data by airline companies falls in the category of data protection (Unwatched 2007 : 3). And the yet-to-be-adopted framework decision regulates the exchange of data between member states – not the national laws of member states, which means that "(i)n effect there will be no data protection law regulating the national collection and processing of the data" (Statewatch 2007 : 8).

Although the proposal said in Article 3.2 that data revealing racial or ethnic origin would be deleted by the Passenger Information Unit, and the persons in charge were stressing that ethnic profiling would not be involved, some members of the European Parliament were still concerned that racial profiling could still occur (Fay 2007 : 2). Names and addresses may reveal a lot about a person's ethnicity. Professor Takis Takimidis of Matrix Chambers said that the planned 'positive profiling' could be a disguised way of racial profiling:

> "For instance if the authorities only profile those who have Asian names. But if they profile everybody who is a passenger, I can't see what could be wrong with this. But it's very hard to say whether positive profiling would be problematic without knowing exactly what it is." (Travis 2006 : 2)

For instance, the American Federal Aviation Administration insists that their Computer Assisted Passenger Pre-Screening (CAPPS) does not target any group based on race, national origin or religion. "But there have been complaints that Arab Americans and Muslims have been disproportionately selected by the system" (BBC 2001a : 2). Furthermore it could be the case that passengers flying to or from destinations classified as 'high-risk countries' are disproportionately profiled. In addition to that, diplomats said that sensitive data, as described in art 3.2 of the proposal, can be exceptionally used when it "(…) could save the life of the passenger or somebody else's" (AP 2007 : 1)[12].

[12] A similar statement is available at the website of the BNET Security Roundup

EU Justice and Security Commissioner Franco Frattini said that he would propose two further schemes to collect travelers' data, which propose a register collecting biometric information on all non-EU travelers entering and leaving the 27-nation bloc, plus a check on all air passengers with a form which is to be filled in on the Internet some days before traveling (Melander 2008 : 1).

3.6 Further Possible Scenarios of Ethnic Profiling and Modern Security Technology

Since 2004 European ministers have been exploring possibilities for uniform airport security checks, since security technology, as well as agreements on security checks still vary from country to country. Identifying passengers by biometric data, such as fingerprints or other physical markers is limited to frequent travelers in some nations. British Home Secretary John Reid argues for higher security standards on airports: "As we face the threat of mass murder, we have to accept that the rights of the individual that we enjoy must and will be balanced with the collective right of security and the protection of life and limb that our citizens demand" (Stinson 2006 : 1).

One of the early measures after 9/11 was the introduction of biometric passports, which was enacted in December 2004. Biometric data, like digital photos and fingerprints, is meant to help improve the security standards of passports: it allows the verification of the authenticity of the document and the identity of the holder (Europa.eu 2006 : 1), although identification systems, which rely on PINs and ID cards etc., only identify PINs and cards, not real people. In other words: when a correct card is shown or scanned by the system, this simply means that someone carries the correct card, who might or might not be the authorized user (O'Connor 2002 : 167).

A further measure would be the use of biometric data in boarding cards to verify if the person who checked in at the counter is the same person boarding the plane (Junge 2008 : 1). For the same reason some airports have already installed a fingerprint check-in option. There are many automated ID-verification systems working in a similar manner: hand geometry

- Air Safety Week. Available at: http://findarticles.com/p/articles/mi_m0UBT/is_30_21/ai_n27333947

measurement, iris scanning, retinal scanning, or gait recognition[13]. Other electromagnetic wave based technologies are already in use, for instance metal detectors, x-rays and radio frequency IDs[14]. Almost all of these examples do not contain information on a person's ethnicity or religion. As long as they are applied with every passenger (and not disproportionately), a misuse of this information in terms of ethnic profiling is not very likely. But as already pointed out, this depends on the information saved in the microchip in Radio Frequency IDs and the usage of biometric data in ID cards or boarding passes. Data about a person's ethnicity could be misused: "Biometric identifications are only as fair and objective as the political intentions behind them. Unfairly applied, they may compound, rather than eliminate existing stereotypes and prejudices" (Zalman 2008b : 1).

Security technology, such as body scanning as well as facial recognition could entail more problems in terms of ethnic profiling. Facial recognition software relies on mapping key facial features and creates a unique 'faceprint': eyes, nose, mouth, front etc. are measured as well as their relative position to each other. However, the faces of those whom someone would like to protect himself from have to be entered in a database first (O'Connor 2002 : 153). A match is assumed when a certain threshold of shared values in the two 'faceprints' have been reached. Facial recognition software is designed to pick out potential terrorists of a crowd and it is already installed on numerous airports. As opposed to 'verification tools' (the system compares a new sample to a sample in a database), facial recognition is an 'identification tool' and conducts a 'one to many'-match wherein a new

---

[13] Researchers at the Georgia Institute of Technology are developing technologies to recognize a person's walk, or gait. Results indicate these new identification methods hold promise as tools in the war on terrorism and in medical diagnosis (Sanders 2002 :1).

[14] Radio Frequency Identification (RFID) technology uses radio waves to identify objects and people. The identification system consists of a RFID reader and a RFID tag, which could be attached to ID cards or goods. The Department of Homeland Security is currently testing the use of RFID tags for foreign visitors coming through Arizona, New York, and Washington State. Visitors are assigned tags upon entry that track their border crossings. The U.S. promises that the tags will not contain biometric or other identifying information, and that the serial codes will only be legible to government recording devices (Zalman 2008a : 1).

sample is presented to the system and the system must compare it with all the templates in the database, but – again – the system does not recognize anyone for whom no information (e.g., a photograph) has been entered into the system previously. And we have either no pictures, no picture detailed enough of a terrorist yet, or we do not know who some of them are (Ibid. : 164f). Apart from the fact that the system itself is not immune to security attacks – sophisticated individuals could circumvent the system by hacking the network, using some sort of prosthetic device to mimic the physical characteristics to be scanned etc. (Ibid. : 166) – the system can easily be misused for ethnic profiling. Even though facial recognition may primarily be used for descriptive profiling, some systems may be programmed to classify screened individuals by skin color or other distinguishing features. In combination with a predictive ethnic profile, the system could be the most 'adequate' instrument to implement ethnic profiling.

A different popular kind of monitoring focuses on behavioral aspects: since 2004 project 'Safee'[15] is being developed on behalf of the European Commission. With it the new level of control in counter-terrorism is prepared and researchers are testing future possibilities – excluding political or ethical concerns for now. Real-time localization is one example of a camera surveillance program tested in Debrecen, Hungary: a microchip implanted in the boarding card makes it possible for cameras and microphones to detect everyone at any time – everywhere on the airport. The data is transmitted to a facial expression-program developed by behavioral psychologists. If this program analyzes danger, sky marshals are precautionarily informed (Junge 2008 : 1). As long as the system monitors and analyzes every person and not a disproportionate selection, it could circumvent ethnic profiling – but equally invades everyone's privacy thoroughly [16].

---

[15] 'Safee' encompasses the development and testing of several new security technologies: a sensor in the plane toilets' sink detects the mixing of Chemicals, which again is connected to a camera system; another project is the tele-control of hijacked airplanes that conducts the plane from the terrain (Junge 2008 : 1f).

[16] Another question is how general fear of flying could be misinterpreted by the system as a 'dangerous nervousness'.

Data Mining

Data mining is a version of artificial intelligence[17]. Large volumes of data can be analyzed and searched for yet unknown patterns by using genetic algorithms[18]. The results of this analysis can be used as a prediction instrument to build models on real world behavior, which are again used in counter-terrorism for preventive reasons. Any kind of database can be used for data mining, such as library lists, official registers, collected data in stores, or e-mails. Sweden, for example, passed in June 2008 a controversial surveillance bill, which allows all cross-border Internet- and telephone-communication to be monitored in the name of national security. This data could also be used for data mining. The law is set to take effect on Jan. 1, 2009. The Swedish government cited "(…) the changing nature of security threats, terrorism, international crime and the specter of cyber warfare to push through the law" (DW-World 2008 : 1).

However, using data mining in counter-terrorism involves diverse problems: firstly, it is not very likely that there is enough data fed into the analytic system to allow indicating patterns of terrorist behavior. Since terrorist attacks are extremely rare, they follow the logic of a one- or two-time-event rather than a pattern:

> "For example, if we were to build a model predicting a terrorist attack based on 9/11, we might create a model that would correlate male Arab men who had attended flight school with purchase of

[17] Artificial intelligence (AI) programs are designed to process and analyze huge amounts of data. AI computer programs mimic human intelligence "(...) not only by performing the same functions that humans do (like recognizing speech), but by being able to either reason or learn from examples" (Zalman 2008c : 1).

[18] Genetic algorithms are computer-based calculations that rely on the evolutionary survival-of-the-fittest-principle. A large set of data can be winnowed down to the data that 'fit' the most to a particular problem. In counter-terrorism genetic algorithms are used to "(e)xtract the fittest nodes (or connection points) in terrorist networks, in order to analyze and act on that knowledge; Determine the most optimal military or other strategy to use in a particular scenario. "fitness" in this case is determined as the ability to resolve a violent conflict scenario; Create models of new threat scenarios by 'evolving' the most dangerous scenarios from component parts (fitness in this case means the ability to survive existing strategies for their defeat)" (Zalman 2008d : 1)

> airline tickets. But there is no evidence whatever that this behavior is a pattern, rather than a one time event." (Zalman 2008e : 1)

There is probably a higher chance of finding a pattern that indicates a terrorist cell rather than predicting an attack. Furthermore, terrorists could defeat an assumed pattern by acting differently.

The EU member states and Europol have increased data sharing to develop a terrorist profile. However, there is the possibility to abuse data mining to develop a terrorist profile including information on ethnicity, the EU Network of Independent Experts in Fundamental Rights pointed out that there has to be a "(…) statistically significant demonstration of the relations between these characteristics and the risk of terrorism" (Goldston 2006 : 6).

The Example of the German Dragnet Investigation

Horst Herold, former director of the German Federal Criminal Police Office (BKA), introduced a system similar to data mining called dragnet investigation (Rasterfahndung), in the 1970s. As opposed to data mining in its original sense, a dragnet investigation does not generate a pattern, but works on the basis of a previously determined profile. Existing databases are screened upon that particular profile and its logic nexus. The intersection, or the so-called 'sediments', of the screened data is then prosecuted with normal law enforcement techniques. There are two kinds of dragnet investigations: winnowing a data set gradually to find yet unknown suspects is called negative dragnet investigation. Positive dragnet investigation, however, involves searching databases for known suspects (Grötker 2002 : 1f).

In the 1970s German police used addresses and license numbers to conduct dragnet investigations. Today's data sets give information about almost every area of life. As per resolution and the German 'Terrorismusbekämpfungsgesetz' from 2002, it is allowed to investigate registers e.g. of aliens departments, universities, banks, telecommunication companies and registration offices (Ibid. : 2).

Between 2001 and 2003 a German dragnet investigation took place to identify potential terrorist 'sleeper cells'. Sensitive personal data of approximately 8.3 million persons was collected from public and private databases. The profile was based on the characteristics of members of the 'Hamburg cell' including: 18-40 years old, male, current or former student, resident in the regional state (Land) the data is collected in, Muslim, legal residency in Germany, nationality or country of birth from a list of 26 states with predominantly Muslim population or stateless person or nationality 'undefined' or 'unknown'. These criteria did deliberately involve information on ethnicity. Finally, the sleeper database contained approximately 32,000 data entries. Some were singled out for further police investigation, but generally the amount of data was still too much to follow-up for the police. In order to cut that number down, additional data was collected from persons who had received information relevant for a terrorist attack. The individuals singled out were for example monitored and interrogated. Eventually, not a single terrorist suspect was identified (OSI 2007 : 8).

Klaus Rogall, a German professor of criminal law, participated in the process of making dragnet investigation a legal research instrument for the police in the 1970s. He claimed that there was no reason to be worried about the dragnet investigation of 2001-2003, since the fact of corresponding to a certain characteristic trait thus setting off the process of being monitored, would be completely coincidental (Grötker 2002 : 3). On the other hand data protectors argued that individual freedom was already impaired by the possibility to be monitored by the police.

However, in 2006 the dragnet investigation after the 9/11 attacks was judged illegal, since it was used as a precautionary measure. Preventive dragnet investigations are generally justified when objects of legal protection, such as the security of the union or a person's life, freedom or physical condition, are in immediate danger. General external tensions, as there were after the 9/11 attacks, do not justify a dragnet investigation (Nowak 2006 : 1).

Furthermore, the profile used for that specific investigation was based on sensitive data involving ethnicity, which put the majority of members of a certain ethnic group under general suspicion. This was similarly described by Christian Berg, spokesman of the 'Freier Zusammenschluss von StudentInnenschaften' in Gemany:

> "Das Urteil macht deutlich, dass die Bundesrepublik mit den Grundrechten ausländischer Studierender nicht umspringen kann, wie sie möchte. Ausländische Studierende, vornehmlich aus arabischen Ländern, wurden unter Generalverdacht gestellt und waren monatelang unter den absurdesten Umständen polizeilicher Willkür und dem Misstrauen ihrer Kommilitoninnen und Kommilitonen ausgesetzt." (Ibid. : 2)[19]

[19] (Rough translation) "The judgment makes clear that the German government cannot treat the rights of immigrant students arbitrarily. Foreign students, primarily from Arab countries, were under general suspicion and were exposed to the most absurd circumstances of arbitrariness by the police and the distrust of their fellow students."

4. POSSIBLE IMPLICATIONS OF ETHNIC PROFILING

A conclusion that can be drawn from the different examples in the last chapter is that there are two main attitudes towards the inclusion of sensitive data in profiling for counter-terrorism purposes. Those in favor refer to the relative success of what adherents generally call ethnic or racial profiling[1]. Both camps have weighty arguments for their positions and since the topic is generally considered delicate, both parties' arguments include scientific references. The effectiveness of this method cannot and shall not be empirically tested within the scope of this paper, but different implications of ethnic profiling shall be exposed in the next few chapters. There are many ways to categorize these implications: authors refer to short- and long-term effects, and to positive and negative impacts. The categories introduced in this thesis, however, are primary and secondary effects. They cover other aspects than the categories mentioned before, making them the more suitable for the use in this paper.

Primary effects consider the direct outcome of the measure in question, such as averted attacks or arrest and detention in the direct aftermath of the implementation of ethnic profiling. Most of the law enforcement statistics are quoted in this context to confirm the effectiveness of ethnic profiling. Primary effects are generally taken into account in a policy of deterrence or incapacitation.

Secondary effects focus on long-term effects, such as implications on social life. Such implications are rarely considered in security policy, not least because they are difficult to detect and quantify. Their impact is at first speculative or theoretical, since a less distinct group is affected. Other secondary effects concern the methodology of ethnic profiling. Some errors in reasoning might lead to considerable breaches in the theoretical basis and practice of ethnic profiling. Thus, the argument of this thesis is that secondary effects should produce repercussions on security policy, too, and shall therefore be outlined and discussed with reference to examples of European counter-terrorism taken form articles, scientific studies or books.

[1] Once more: to simplify matters, the term ethnic profiling is used throughout this thesis, without implying a political position.

4.1 The Deterring Effects of Ethnic Profiling

It is clear that profiling has various effects on criminal offenders as well as on crime rates. The most prominent of these is deterrence, which will be explained later in this chapter. Deterrence is not only an important component of modern criminal policy, but plays a fundamental role in the everyday life of the police. Consequently, the use of terrorist profiling may come about in many ways. It can occur informally, for example when police officers rely on their own sets of characteristics when deciding whom to stop and search for counter-terrorism reasons. This is known to happen – whether authorized or not (Moeckli 2006 : 5)[2]. However, after 9/11 the deployment of profiles has increasingly become a conscious political decision. Former New York City[3] Police Commissioner Howard Safir comments that not taking ethnicity into account would simply be irresponsible. He gives reasons for the described rising deployment of profiles in counter-terrorism:

> "We know that the 19 (9-11) hijackers were Middle-Eastern men between 18 and 23. We know that the people who hit the Cole were the same profile. We know that the people who hit the embassies in Africa were the same profile. So not using what we know--that the probability that a Middle-Eastern male between 18 and 23 is going to be a terrorist--not using that, is folly. And I think we should use it. But it's not racial profiling, it's terrorist profiling." (Stakelbeck 2007 : 1)

New Tendencies: The Deployment of Ethnic and Terrorist Profiling in European Counter-Terrorism

Safir's arguments are reflected in European counter-terrorism policies as well. New amendments, which tighten European anti-terror laws, as well as security plans on a national level indicate a tendency toward the use of profiling and provide wider powers for security personnel. Some measures

---

2 q.v. 2.1 on the genesis of criminal profiling

3 Drawing on American Police Officers' or American Politics' statements in this thesis shall not contradict the fact that the main focus of this thesis is Europe. Such quotations are implied to clarify or typify some general lines of argument that are not necessarily bound to a certain continents' counter-terrorism strategy or security policy.

and laws may be considered a precursor for the use of sensitive data in counter-terrorism.

For example, the national security statement made by the British Prime Minister in November 2007 pronounced restrictions in border control and wider cooperation between border control agencies and those making visa-decisions overseas. Henceforth the protection of borders against possible terrorists would also be among the duties of border control staff, which underscores the assumption that possible terrorist threats come from outside the nation's borders:

> "To ensure that we protect our borders and detect possible terrorist suspects, members of the new UK border agency will have the power, from January next year, to detain people not just on suspicion of immigration offences or for customs crime but for other criminal activity, including terrorism. Powers will also be given to airline liaison officers to cancel visas when justified." (Brown 2007 : 3)

Furthermore, the Prime Minister also envisaged biometric visas for all applicants and biometric ID cards for foreign nationals. Similar plans have been put forth by the EU through the Schengen Information System II (SIS II) which also incorporates biometric data. Through the introduction of biometric visas and data, the amount of information made available for profiling rises.

In addition to that, a new border protection system, supported by Frontex[4], is intended to protect the EU against illegal immigration and spot people within the EU with expired visas. Furthermore it provisions profiling by means of European police databases to detect and combat terrorism as well as illegal immigration. These profiles contain information on ethnicity, race, religion and nationality. In spite of the citicism that potential terrorists are not likely to be detected by means of such a profile, the work on a European 'mega-database' continues. It is very likely that Frontex will be the central agency in this context (Heilig 2008 : 1).

The initiative of establishing terrorist profiling throughout the EU already existed in November 2002, when the Council of the European Union published a recommendation, which envisioned cooperation between Europol

---

4 European Agency for the Management of Operational Cooperation at the External Borders

and immigration authorities to identify terrorists before a terrorist act would be carried out, as well as identifying persons and environments significant for the recruitment of terrorists (Council of the European Union Document 11858/3/02 : 2ff.). Several EU member states, among them Germany and Great Britain, collaborated with Europol to put together "(…) a set of physical, psychological or behavioural variables, which have been identified, as typical of persons involved in terrorist activities and which may have some predictive value in that respect" (Ibid. : 5). This was supposed to lead to individual profiles of persons who fulfill particular functions in a specialized category of terrorism (Ibid. : 6). According to the document a terrorist profile is based on "(…) information of a non-personal nature" (Ibid. : 3), but it might include data on the nationality, travel document, method and means of travel, age, sex, distinguishing physical features, education, choice of cover identity, places of stay, place of birth, psycho-sociological features etc. (Ibid. : 6f). The results were, and apparently still are to be used in cooperation with immigration authorities and the police. The profiles are meant to be updated as often as possible. The authors of the paper acknowledge that establishing a single terrorist profile is not possible, as terrorism as a world-wide phenomenon is complex and the characteristics of organizations involved in terrorism, as well as their respective participants, differ greatly (Ibid. : 6f). In doing so, it is left to the government and the law enforcement agencies to identify or define the kind of terrorism worth concentrating on, and consequently the composition of the profile and whether it should contain group characteristics such as race or religion[5]. As it says in the paper, most member countries were already working on a terrorist profile (Ibid. : 5).

---

[5] Amy Zalman gives an overview of the different categories of terrorist groups. First she mentions pre-modern groups. They are not understood as part of the modern terrorism (which is considered the struggle between non-state organizations and modern states). Pre-modern groups are the Hashhashin, Sicarly and Thugees. The second category, socialist or communist terrorism, aims at the socialist revolution. Groups, such as the Baader-Meinhof Group (Germany), PFLP (Palestine), Red Brigades (Italy), Revolutionary Struggle (Greece) or Shining Path (Peru) mostly arose in the last half of the 20th century. The ETA (Basque), Fatah (Palestine), Irgun (Zionist), IRA (Ireland), PKK (Kurdistan) or Tamil Tigers (Sri Lanka) contest national liberation – one of the most potent reasons for groups to employ violence while fighting for their goals. Religious-political or religious-

In addition to these plans, the EU just recently tightened its anti-terrorism laws, for example by punishing incitement to terrorism through the internet and by establishing an early warning system connected to that (BBC NEWS 2008a : 1). But it is not only the new political measures and laws, which may be considered a precursor for the use of information on ethnicity in profiling. The method itself is considered effective: as the former police commissioner Howard Safir pointed out, a main argument is that race is a significant factor for profiling and deterring terrorists successfully.

Race as a Relevant Factor

As a general rule all airports within the European Union, if not throughout the world, conduct random searches for security reasons, mostly in connection with the use of metal detectors. This randomized search could generally apply to every passenger, on some airports every single passenger is screened by a metal detector. The fact that random searches are the most appropriate solution to implement security measures in a non-discriminatory way is self-explanatory. However, some politicians and authors point out that focusing on a high-offender population in such security measures is necessary to not waste energy. High-offenders are in this case members of a minority group in Europe and such a practice would legitimize singling out specific ethnic groups. Stephen J. Ellmann from the New York Law School emphasizes that law-enforcement officials should focus on a high-offending group and not waste energy with randomized searches:

> "Early in 2002, my daughter, who was 6 years old at the time and traveling with her mother, was selected this way. Her backpack was opened and searched, and she was subjected to a metal detector wand and patdown search of her body. (…) (I)t isn't conceivable

---

nationalist terrorism involves a combination of a religious mission and political goals, such as recognition, power, territory etc. Abu Sayyaf (Philippines/Islamist), Al Quaeda (transnational/Islamist), Aum Shinrikyo (renamed Aleph, Japanese/inc. Hindu, Buddhist), Egyptian Islamic Jihad, Hamas (Palestine/Islamist), Hezbollah (often referred to as a movement, rather than a terrorist group), Klu Klux Klan (U.S./Christian), Palestinian Islamic Jihad and the Salafist Group for Preaching and Combat (Algeria/Islamist) belong to the religious-political category. The last and most controversial category is terrorism committed by a State. Some States or State actions, however, are considered State terrorism, such as the Nazi-Germany or Stalinist Russia. (Zalman 2008f : 1f).

> that 6-year-old girls pose the same threat to airline security (…) that grown men do. So if six-year-olds are actually as likely to be randomly searched as grown men are, then some substantial amount of law-enforcement effort is being largely wasted, as far as preventing terrorist attacks is concerned." (Ellmann 2003 : 686)

He does however argue that a certain proportion of random searches would still make sense to dissuade those who would seek to slip through the profile. In his view, so as not to waste energy, security policy personnel has three profiling options: a) including race, religion and similar factors, b) selecting people solely based on behavioral aspects, such as nervousness, lack of round-trip ticket or c) including both kind of variables. Referring to the context of ethnic profiling in drug trafficking, he says that the success of ethnic profiling depends on the situation and only makes sense when ethnicity is combined with other factors.

> "It could be inferred, then, that by using race plus other factors, police were able to select a much larger group of drivers, included both blacks and whites, for productive search than they would have been able to had they excluded race from consideration altogether." (Ibid. : 702)

Even if his suggestion gets very close to what randomization actually is, he still advocates the inclusion of race, religion, national origin and gender along with individual behavioral characteristics, if any of these characteristics are relevant – even if it is considered discriminatory (Ibid. : 695f). According to him, these characteristics are relevant, if they help in a 1:1000 chance to identify a terrorist. In this case ethnic profiling is justified, since it can be considered an effective tool (Ibid. : 699ff)[6].

In the terrorism-context it is assumed that the high-offending group consist of young Muslim men, who look Middle-Eastern, South-East Asian or North African. Women, older men and young white men belong to the non-profiled group. According to the number of committed attacks by members of the profiled group, this assumption is probably true. There are only very

[6] Considering possible secondary effects of profiling he concludes that in the context of stop and searches they are almost none: "The isolation and potential danger in highway stops and street stop-and-frisks should be absent. These intrusions are not trivial, but their impact should not be exaggerated either" (Ellman 2003 : 709).

few cases of when people of the non-profiled group planned an attack, for example Richard Reid, a British-Jamaican, who was known as the 'shoe bomber'. In opposition to that, the nineteen men who participated in the 9/11 attacks were Muslim. The share of this group in European society is much smaller than the share of the non-targeted group[7], so one can indeed say that there is a significant offending differential (Harcourt 2006 : 14f). The actual number of young Muslim men who committed attacks in Europe depends on what kind of terrorism one focuses on. However, considering the terrorist attacks of the last ten years, it is true that the people responsible for the London bombings or the attacks in Madrid were members of al Quaeda. This being said, there is a tendency towards 'deploying' people for attacks, who do not fit the characteristics typically used in ethnic profiling (s. chapter 4.2).

According to Ellmann, the argument that makes ethnicity a relevant factor is that the potential terrorist is an enemy the state is at war with. And those potential enemies do belong to a certain ethnic group, which automatically makes them a higher-offending group. This again represents so grave a risk that the state, in this case the US "(…) must commit the nation to finding and killing them if they do not surrender" (Ibid. : 684). One fact that he does not take into account is that there is a fairly big Muslim community in the US, which makes it improbable to be able to distinguish between Muslims who are US citizens from and Muslims from abroad that are hostile towards the US. Furthermore, Ellmann conflates religion and race, which both represent very different characteristics that could be drawn upon in ethnic profiling (more about the conflation of race and religion in chapter 4.2). In addition to that, no country in Europe that considers taking race into account in their national counter-terrorism is literally 'at war'. The war-argument seemed nevertheless to be very present in US politics – even six years after the 9/11 attacks: New York Assemblyman Dov Hikind assumed that the fear of offending people of a certain descent could bar politicians from racial profiling of potential terrorists. He proposed legislation to make what he calls 'terrorist profiling' legal: "Radical Islam believes that killing Americans – killing, murdering Westerners – is fulfilling God's will. When you are fighting that kind of war, you can't be politically correct" (Stakelbeck 2007 : 1).

---

[7] Of course this is only true for the US or Europe.

Concerning this kind of 'war against terror', different authors refer to the profile of the al Quaeda-members responsible for the 9/11 attacks. This profile primarily includes 'male' and 'of Middle Eastern origin'. Group membership is used as a relevant factor and in this case this factor derives from a descriptive profile. Ellmann argues that

> "(i)n the context of terrorism, it is similarly impossible to ignore the fact (…) that we have been attacked by a Muslim terrorist organization with roots in Arab states. This fact, and people's reactions to it, will shape our law enforcement response whether we acknowledge it or not." (Ellmann 2003 : 705)

Apart from the fact that ethnic profiling may occur 'whether acknowledged or not', it is important to consider the function of descriptive profiling in counter-terrorism. In the debate on the deployment of ethnic profiling, descriptive profiling has an exceptional position. As we already considered earlier, taking existing characteristics into account in the aftermath of a criminal offense is inevitable, if not essential, in law enforcement:

> "When police have information that a crime they are investigating was committed by someone belonging to a particular ethnic or religious group, it will generally be perfectly reasonable and legitimate for them to use this information for a suspect description." (Moeckli 2006 : 14)

For example, in 2007 the CIA provided the German secret services with information on terrorists hiding in Oberschledorn, who then were successfully arrested. One of these terrorists was of Middle Eastern descent (Peters 2007 : 1f). If the CIA used ethnic profiling in this specific case is unclear – presumably the German secret services finally took advantage of the descriptive profiles of these particular terrorists.

In many cases however, descriptive profiling in counter-terrorism is structurally used as predictive profiling, for example when elements of al Quaeda terrorist profiles are generally used in the context of preempting terrorism, even though it is not clear whether al Quaeda is actually planning an attack. Even though this might happen in an informal rather than a formal context of policing and profiling, it is questionable if – what this thesis refers to as indirect predictive profiling – can be justified with the same arguments (s. chapter 4.2).

The Rationale of Profiling

Criminal profiling entails shifting the focus of law enforcement to a high-offending group of a certain kind of crime – in this case terrorist activities. According to the laws of probability, exerting criminal profiling then leads to the increased detection of offenders in the direct aftermath of a crime since simply more law enforcement personnel is dedicated to detecting the targeted group.

Therefore the claim that the success of profiling is statistically proven, is generally justifiable for the narrow time span following the implementation of profiling. For this reason the proponents' main argument for terrorist profiling is indeed sustainable. The advantage of profiling is that there is not even necessarily more personnel needed, but simply the increased sampling from a high-offending group leads to an increased success rate. A further determinant in this context is the frequency of the profiled event: the higher the frequency, the higher the probability of detecting these events or offenders. The benefits of the increased detection of terrorists in the immediate aftermath of profiling are a) that the actual attack is averted, and b) that through incapacitation of the offender future attacks are prevented. Of course, the immediate detection of terrorists is of great importance to potential victims and the families of those victims (Harcourt 2006 : 11f).

However, it is important that the group trait, which is part of the profile, is indeed statistically proven to correlate with the particular offense. The case that a correlation does indeed exist is also called 'statistical discrimination'. It is necessary to make sure that the profiled group is indeed a high- or higher-offending group, which presupposes some substantiated research work before profiling. Thankfully terrorism is a low-base rate event (Harcourt 2006 : 12), but this also implies that there is not as much data to draw upon as in other categories of criminal offenses.

Theoretical Foundation: Rational Choice & Target Hardening

As already pointed out above, profiling is a strategy to enhance the efficiency of policing and can therefore be referred to as an economic model. The most famous economic theory of crime is the rational choice theory, which is based on the assumption that "(...) people will engage in crime after weighing the costs and benefits of their actions to arrive at a rational choice about motivation after perceiving that the chances of gain outweigh any possible punishment or loss (O'Connor 2006 : 7)."

The continuation of this theory is the Routine Activity Approach, namely the idea that "(…) a criminal act has three minimal elements: a likely offender, a suitable target, and the absence of capable guardians against crime" (Felson 1986 : 121). Even though Felson considers the 'capable guardian' rather as informally connected to the offender, it may also be a police officer or a security watchman who keeps the offender from committing a crime. The guardian or another security measure can be part of keeping the target safe, which criminologists refer to as 'target hardening'. All these are components of deterrence policy.

In 1999, Dean Rasinya, former captain of the New York City Police Department answered a series of readers' comments on racial profiling, which he refers to as a legitimate policing strategy of target hardening:

"What you call racial profiling, I refer to as target hardening. Gender, race and age are three of the many demographics police officers use to eliminate people from the mix of who may be stopped for questioning. (…) A thorough knowledge of the area you work in is necessary – who lives and visits there, the socioeconomic makeup, physical layout, types of crime occurring. This information is part of the target-hardening (or profiling) process that takes place long before an officer sets foot on the gas pedal. It is my belief that the process of target hardening is a series of mental steps that eliminate those whom the police are not looking for, thus leaving a relatively small portion of the community for scrutiny." (Rasinya 1999 : 1)

The two models of rational reasoning, rational choice and routine activity, can be applied to the concept of committing – or averting, a terrorist attack. Security measures such as ethnic profiling can be a form of target hardening that makes terrorists refrain from executing their plans. O'Connor gives some more factors influencing the rational choice of terrorism, namely place, size and time:

> "A terrorist plot in a democratic society is less likely to involve senseless violence than a scheme hatched under an authoritarian regime because under the latter, terrorists realize they have nothing to lose with the expected repercussions. Size is important because a small elite group is more likely to resort to terrorism when the

> population is passive. This means that more senseless acts of violence may occur in a stable society rather than one on the verge of collapse. Time constraints are important because the terrorist group may be competing with other groups or attempting to manage a tit-for-tat strategy with counterterrorism." (O'Connor 2006 : 8)

However, the exact reasons why terrorists abandon a potential attack after having weighed the consequences are obviously not testable. The 'cost' factor of being caught and punished could be one aspect, however the potential 'cost' of not reaching their original aim of a 'successful mission' could weigh heavily against that. Since many terrorists are willing to give their own lives to complete a mission, the fear of being punished for their committed crime afterwards does probably not deter them from committing the attack. For these individuals the possibility of failing the mission and being caught by law enforcement could be more of a deterrent.

The process of terrorists refraining from their original plans, since the 'cost' of committing the attack was increased by the chance of being caught through ethnic profiling, is called 'elasticity of offending to policing'. It is the degree to which changes in policing affect changes in offending – here: committing a terrorist attack. (Harcourt 2006 : 13). So provided that terrorists do respond rationally to increased target hardening, i.e. ethnic profiling, then by targeting the high-offending group, law enforcement officers will not only detect more terrorist activities, but terrorists may also refrain from their plans. The result of these primary effects would be an overall decrease of terrorist attacks or activities.

> "In its purest from, the economic model of crime suggests that law enforcement should target higher offending populations until the point where their offending rates have fallen to the same level as the general population. At that point, the government maximizes the effectiveness of its law enforcement resources." (Ibid. : 13)

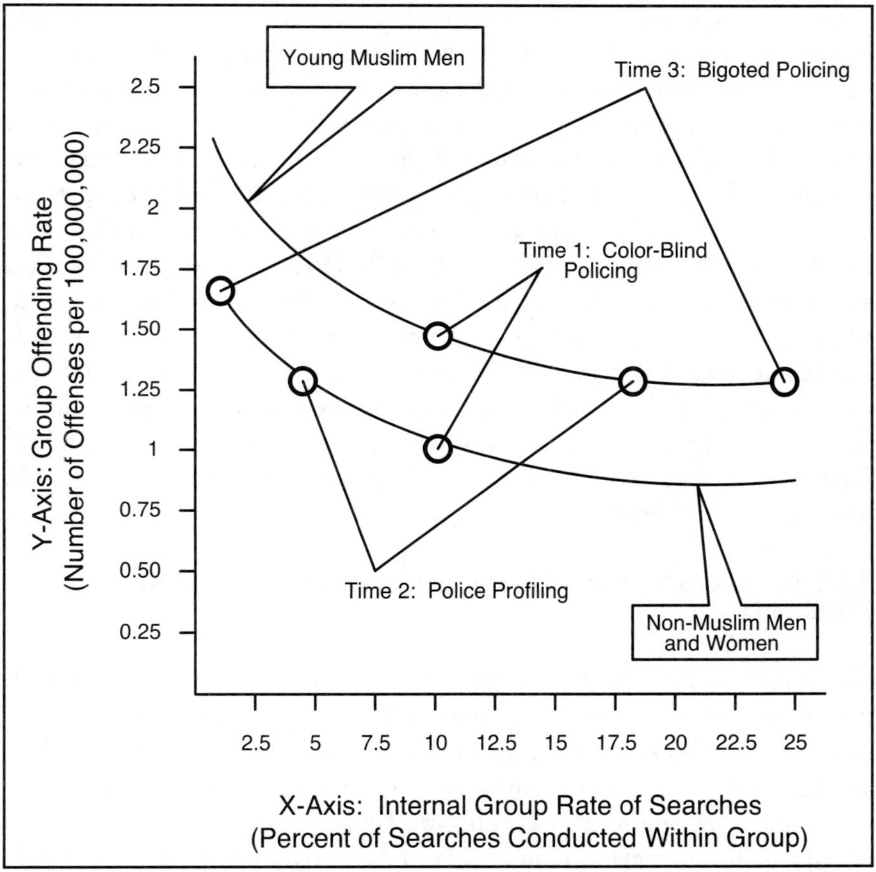

Fig. 2: The Economic Model of Profiling (Harcourt 2006 : 17)

To explain and visualize the effectiveness of (ethnic) profiling Harcourt developed this graph: at Time 1 the police is not using profiles at all. They search both groups, the high-offending minority group (young Muslim men) and white men and women, at the same internal search rate of 10 percent. However, the graph reflects the assumption of non-spurious profiling: as opposed to white men and women, young Muslim men are offending at a 1.5 versus 1 per 100 million rate. This results in slightly more successful searches of young Muslim men, which again prompts police officers to enhance their search rate for this group, even though the number of the searches is higher than their share of the available population. According to the rational choice theory the offending rate of young Muslim men then decreases somewhat proportionally to the increase of the searches. Due to this success, the offending rate of this group drops to the level of that of white men and women – the non-profiled group (Time 2). The police now engage in profiling and search about 18% of the available young Muslim men and 5% of the available white men and women, which results in a hypothetical total distribution of 60/40. Offending rates and hit rates are similar at that distribution of searches. Since the number of successful searches has now increased and the level of the targeted group's offending has decreased (from Time 1) the officer has no reason to change the distribution of searches (Ibid. : 15). Some proponents believe that with the decrease of the targeted-group's offending, the total societal level of offending decreases, too. This however, is questionable and not reflected in the graph (s. next chapter).

4.2 The Concept of Ethnic Profiling and its Methodological Weaknesses

Given that most of the prevailing and well-known terrorists are of Arab provenance or of Muslim appearance, reliance on the adherent characteristics seems to make intuitive sense. The police can only employ profiling effectively as long as there is information on the appearance or behavior of the suspects (q.v. descriptive profiling). However, despite the evidentiary arguments for the balanced and successful deployment of ethnic profiling, the concept contains some far-reaching methodological breaches. Terrorist profiles are often designed to find so-called 'sleepers', individuals that may not fit certain patterns, since their existence is only assumed (Moeckli 2006 : 6ff). The document of the Council of the European Union itself says that the profiles are designed to identify terrorists before an act is carried out (Council of the European Union Document 11858/3/02: 7). The fact that elements of a descriptive profile are used to find yet unknown sleepers, poses a challenge for terrorist profiling or may even question the method itself, because it reveals itself as indirect predictive profiling, which uses ex post-elements ex ante.

It is mostly predictive profiles which are needed to prevent future attacks, descriptive profiles are often not very useful in the context of terrorism:

the likelihood that profiling is implemented in the aftermath of very fatal attacks with numerous victims is very high. However, suicide terrorists, for example, die themselves in these kinds of attacks. The aspect of the terrorist's incapacitation to prevent further attacks would not be relevant any longer. The probability that descriptive elements are generalized and summarized in predictive profiles is very high. It is questionable if this is an effective method to find sleepers, since the profile easily becomes too general. The following part exposes this phenomenon in more detail.

Over-Inclusion

Profiling is based on principles that are similar to data mining. In data mining a programmed algorithm finds certain data sets in a huge amount of data. The process is used to find data sets within the data volume matching one prototype-data set ('training set') defined by the researcher. The quality of the prototype-data set and its results depend on the quality and the quantity of data fed into the system. If the algorithm based on the training set is well programmed, it does not simply find meaningful matches, but provides a meaningful percentage-based grading of adequacy of the found data sets. It indicates factors that correlate with the most adequate matches, but were not part of the profile in the first place. In this way data mining may even provide the researcher with new findings on the decisive factors of the profile. However, it is very important that significant factors for the prototype-data set are made out initially so that the system finds significant matches. The process only works if a certain amount of data is fed into the system first. No significant results can be found if the prototype data set itself is based on a too small data volume (and therefore cannot generate significant factors). If the researcher neglects an important factor or puts too much weight on a minor factor, the results of data mining are consequently almost meaningless. In the same manner, profiling relies on a set of significant factors, indicating that certain groups of people pose a greater risk than others. Ethnic profiling acts on the assumption that ethnicity is a significant factor of the profile or the prototype-data set.

The first problem arises with the presumed statistical significance of the factor ethnicity. Predictive profiling practices often rely on broad generalizations of ethnicity or religion. Several authors have pointed out that predictive profiles reflect unexamined or untested preconceptions about ethnicity and religion rather than hard data (Moeckli 2006 : 14)[8]. As already mentioned above, a prototype that is based on deficient factors produces no significant results. A prototype-data set – in this case a profile, should be based on a large amount of data, to find factors that are indeed significant. However, ethnic profiling in counter-terrorism deduces the factor 'Muslim' or 'Arab/ South East Asian' from approximately 45 terrorist data sets, from three main incidents: the 9/11 attacks with 19 suspects, the Madrid bombings with 17 suspects and the London bombings with four suspects (BBC NEWS 2001b : 1, 2005a : 1 & 2005b :1). One can assume that the secret services have included more data sets of individuals involved in averted attacks.

Nevertheless terrorism is luckily a low base-rate event, as already mentioned above. This implicates that the data we have on terrorists is very limited. It is therefore questionable if the totality of data sets used to devise a terrorist profile is enough to find significances for predicting future terrorist attacks. Profiling, however, is at least an attempt to fight terrorism and, according to the EU plan on terrorist profiling, several profiles for different kinds of attacks are devised (Council of the European Union Document 11858/3/02 : 6)[9]. But it is still disputable whether the characteristic 'ethnicity' is significant for predictive profiles based on such a low amount of data sets. Furthermore, it could be instructive to test if there is a correlation of factors (apart from religion) that strict ethnic profiling does not take into account, such as the terrorists' social milieu or distinctive features of their vitas. Only very little research has been done in this field yet. However, the main problem is to infer characteristics from a low amount of data for the prediction of an event that is itself very rare. Knowing these facts, the use of ethnicity as one characteristic in predictive profiling, should be reconsidered.

A second instance that could lead to over-inclusion is the conflation of race and religion in ethnic profiling. Most profiles support the singling out of Muslims, but "(…) since religious affiliation is normally not readily identifiable (and in any case easily concealed), they rely on racial appearance or national origin as proxy traits. Yet race and origin are very poor proxies for religion" (Moeckli 2006 : 15). If we consider the European population we find 455 Million people living in the EU, of which 15 Million are Muslims (dpa 2005 :1). According to a study from 2008, 93 percent of the Muslims

[8] q.v. chapter 5.1 (Werner Schiffauer on the protection of the German constitution)

[9] q.v. chapter 4.1 (on EU terrorist profiling)

worldwide are considered politically moderate and generally support and admire western democratic values. The remaining 7 percent can be considered radical and may tolerate terrorist activities, however this does not necessarily mean that they engage in them (Löhe 2008 : 1).

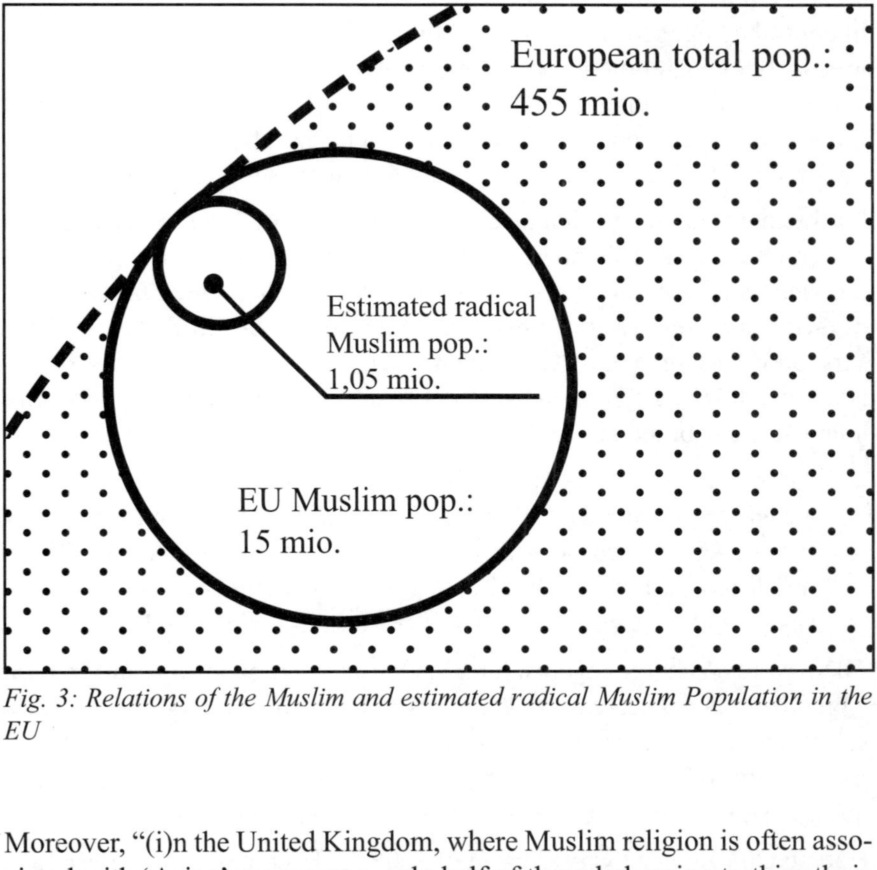

Fig. 3: Relations of the Muslim and estimated radical Muslim Population in the EU

Moreover, "(i)n the United Kingdom, where Muslim religion is often associated with 'Asian' appearance, only half of those belonging to this ethnic group are in fact Muslims" (Moeckli 2006 : 15). This leads to two simple conclusions: first, Muslims do not belong to one ethnic group which could be used as an indicator for being Muslim. Second, only a very small fraction of Muslims are radical at all, which means that if ethnic – or in this case religious – profiling would be implemented consistently and with no consideration of other factors, 93 percent of the profiling would affect innocent people (provided that the 93 percent apply to Muslim men in the same ratio as they do to Muslim women and kids). The conflation of race, nationality or birthplace and religion, as well as the use of religious characteristics as an indicator for being radical Muslim lead to a considerable amount of over-inclusion: people who might match the characteristic of a certain ethnicity might not be Muslim, and if they are, they are not very likely to be engaged in terrorism (Moeckli 2006 : 15). A statistically significant demonstration of a correlation between the factors race or religion and terrorism has not been made at this time (EU Network of Independent Experts in Fundamental Rights 2003 : 21). Therefore, ethnicity and religion in predictive profiling are not suitable means to identify terrorists.

Furthermore, the over-reliance on ethnic appearance has already had serious consequences. The media have reported numerous cases of people being victims of over-anxious counter-terrorism policing. One case with a lot of media attention was the arrest of Ali and Karen Serir in Britain in 2002. Mrs. Serir was three months pregnant when she was detained under Terrorism Act 2000 in an operation to disrupt an alleged plot to bomb Edinburgh's hogmanay celebrations. Her husband allegedly linked to al Quaeda.

> "Mrs. Serir was released after 36 hours in custody and her husband, a chef, was detained by immigration authorities for four months before being released on bail: he is no longer allowed to work. The hogmanay party went ahead with police saying they had no reports suggesting a 'specific' threat." (Gillan/Norton-Taylor/Dodd 2006 : 2)

There were no charges against him. With a deportation to Algeria Mr. Serir would have faced deadly consequences in his home country due to his association to al Quaeda: "There is no doubt that this would put my life at risk if I returned, (…) (t)he Algerian police came to my father's village and questioned him about me, " said Mr. Serir (Green 2003 : 3).

Hocine Ouldzaouche was arrested in 2003 for having planned to use ricin in a gas attack aimed at the London underground:

> "They (the police) told me that I was top of a British intelligence list of terror suspects… I'm a Muslim and totally oppose to terrorism. It was racism and discrimination aimed at Muslims to back the war in Iraq. I was pulled because I was Algerian. They took my books, my photos, my computer. I was released without charge,

> but I still haven't been left alone. The police have turned up where I work. It makes everyone think I'm a terrorist." (Green 2003 : 2)

Yet, eight supposedly extremist Muslims were located together with Mr. Ouldzaouche in the joint French-British police operation in 2003, which prompted UK Prime Minister Tony Blair to emphasize the alert and reality of danger.

In 2005 two British men of Asian descent were wrongfully arrested in connection with the London bombings. Mahammed Rafiq Siddique and Alam Ghafoor were by their own account abused for ten days. Three weeks before, the London Police killed an innocent man of Brazilian descent who was assumed to be a suicide assassin (Spiegel Online 2005 : 1).

Omar Mohammed, a Jordanian living in Coulby Newham, got arrested and released without charge in 2006. His flat and family got searched. His wife's comment on the search gives an insight to what can be perceived as 'suspicious of terrorist activities' by the police:

> "They strip-searched my son Jamie, who was 14, and patted down my daughter who has special needs. She had been scribbling on a piece of junk mail, and it was just squiggles, and they found it and said it was Arabic code. We had a DIY bag with hammers and stuff in it and they said that was bombmaking equipment." (Gillan/Norton-Taylor/Dodd 2006 : 1)

The latest incident happened in 2008 when two politics students got arrested. One of them sent a terror training-manual, part of his research, to a staff member for printing. The police defended the arrest of the two men who were held for six days and later released without charge. The student's tutor explained that the police action was a threat to academic freedom and found the situation especially worrying for those conducting research into terrorism or international security (BBC NEWS 2008b : 1).

The number of 'primary investigative targets' – individuals assumed to be carrying out an attack, rose from about 250 in September 2001 to about 1000 in June 2006. Up to September 2005 895 people have been arrested under Terrorism Act 2000. Only 23 have been convicted of terrorism offences. The main problem is that people are picked on single informant information, which is passed on to the police. However Aamer Anwar, a Scottish human rights lawyer says: "Often, informants are people who are facing threats of deportation or jail or are being given financial assistance. The pressure they put informers under produces misinformation and they will often tell them what they want to hear to stay in the country or stay out of jail" (Gillan/Norton-Taylor/Dodd 2006 : 1).

Another source of information for the police is the secret services, and of course it is almost compulsory to the police to react to that. However, even if passed on by the FBI to the MI5, information can also be incorrect as in the case of the Algerian pilot Lotfi Raissi. He was detained in 2001 on the basis of an FBI tip-off for having been involved in the 9/11 attacks. After five months in the high security Belmarsh prison he was released without any charges connected to terrorism (Green 2003 : 3).

The police insisted that, even though some of the arrested might be innocent and suffer serious consequences because of their arrest, this kind of arrests was necessary to preempt another London bombing, which was – according to officials – very likely in 2006 (Gillan/Norton-Taylor/Dodd 2006 : 1). A member of a British Muslim 'blog' describes the following event:

> "I have a friend that was detained for a few days under the terrorism laws, he had recently completed his PGCE so he could go into teaching after the investigation he was later released without charge. He now has an entry on his CRB Form stating he was arrested for terrorism and he can no longer teach children." (talkislam 2007 : 1)

Even though this information taken from an informal communication on the Internet cannot be proved a genuine event, it might be considered an example of what could happen to innocent people who were detained through over-inclusive ethnic profiling.

Furthermore, it is possible that due to over-inclusion individuals are added to a terrorist watch list, such as the EU list of 'Persons, groups and entities involved in terrorist acts', the UN list of 'individuals and entities associated with al-Quaida or the Taliban' or the UK list of 'international terrorist organisations'. The issues that are related to being listed on one of these indexes cannot be fully discussed in this thesis, but statewatch gives a short summary of the main problems:

> "Groups and individuals are added to the 'terrorist' lists on the basis of 'intelligence' alone. The normal judicial process governing such serious accusations, and their prosecution, has been discarded. (...)

> These lists and the related sanctions are binding on all member states. It is very difficult for those included on the 'terrorist lists' to have their names removed or contest their inclusion. Those in the UK can appeal to a security tribunal (government appointed judges, secret hearing and secret evidence etc.) but the UN and EU lists contain no mechanism of appeal to the courts whatsoever – groups and individuals can only request individual member state governments to make diplomatic representations on their behalf." (statewatch 2005 : 1)

Under-Inclusion

Paradoxically, the over-reliance on ethnic characteristics may also have the opposite effect of what was just described. As already mentioned, the little data we have about terrorists who took part in committing attacks does not necessarily give information about future attackers, since the main unit is too small to make a significant statement about terrorists. It might easily happen that a person who does not match the profile commits an attack.

Furthermore, the success of profiling depends on the kind of terrorism that is supposed to be preempted. A characteristic such as ethnicity does not make sense in a general terrorist profile when the kind of terrorism and its actors differ from the targeted group. One can clarify this with the example of European terrorism: even though European counter-terrorism efforts focus mainly on radical Muslim terrorism, the responsibility for the majority of terrorist attacks in Europe rests with the Basque organization ETA. Radical leftists or separatists are also active in Europe. While the number of arrests generally increased between 2006 and 2008, the number of arrested Muslim radicals declined. However, Islamist terrorists aim at a high number of victims as opposed to separatist terrorism which rather aims at causing damage of property (Europol 2008 : 10ff).

Member state	Islamist	Separatist	Left Wing	Right Wing	Single Issue	Not Specified	Total 2007
Austria	0	0	1	0	0	0	**1**
Denmark	1	0	0	0	0	0	**1**
France	0	253	0	0	0	14	**267**
Germany	1	15	4	0	0	0	**20**
Greece	0	0	2	0	0	0	**2**
Italy	0	0	6	0	0	3	**9**
Portugal	0	0	0	1	1	0	**2**
Spain	0	264	8	0	0	7	**279**
UK	2	–	–	–	–	–	**2**
Total	**4**	**532**	**21**	**1**	**1**	**24**	**583**

Fig. 4: Number of failed, foiled and executed attacks in 2007 per member state and affiliation (Europol 2008 : 10)

Member state	Islamist	Separatist	Left Wing	Right Wing	Single Issue	Total 2007
Austria	5	0	0	3	0	8
Belgium	9	1	0	0	0	10
Bulgaria	4	0	0	0	0	4
Cyprus	2	0	0	0	0	2
Denmark	9	0	0	0	0	9
France	91	315	3	0	0	409
Germany	3	8	4	0	0	15
Ireland	0	24	0	0	0	24
Italy	21	0	23	0	0	44
Portugal	1	0	0	31	0	32
Romania	1	2	0	0	0	3
Slovakia	1	1	0	0	0	2
Spain	48	196	17	0	0	261
Sweden	2	0	0	0	0	2
the Netherlands	4	1	1	10	0	16
UK	–	–	–	–	–	203
Total	**201**	**548**	**48**	**44**	**0**	**1044**

Fig. 5: Number of arrested suspects in 2007 per member state and affiliation (Europol 2008 : 11)

This leads to the conclusion that terrorist profiles should at least differ based on which kind of terrorism they deal with, as for example the document of the Council of the European Union on terrorist profiles is proposing (q.v. 4.1). However, in most cases of European terrorism, ethnicity cannot be considered a striking feature that can be used as a base for distinction, since separatist terrorism may have a lot of different looking actors.

Furthermore, the low frequency of the events leaves terrorist organizations more time to get informed about and adjust to the profile by circumventing it:

> "In the case of low frequency events, the central question is whether the increased likelihood of detection associated with the immediate implementation of a profiling measure will result in the actual detection of planned terrorist activity or instead in the rapid substitution of persons who do not meet the profile or alternative acts that are not as easily profiled." (Harcourt 2006 : 12)

The obvious employment of ethnicity as a factor makes it a lot easier to find ways to avoid being profiled when planning an attack. In this way the over-reliance on ethnic characteristics could also make the officers miss potential terrorists. Such a profile cannot only become self-defeating easily, but it also shifts the law enforcement officers' attention away from behavior, which is a significant factor for finding terrorists (Moeckli 2006 : 16).

There are several ways to consciously evade profiling, yet they are all based on the same principle: substitution. Substitution could be applied on the level of terrorist strategies, instruments or techniques and actors.

Elasticity and Substitution

As members of the profiled group will respond to ethnic profiling, members of the non-profiled group are also changing their behavior. According to the economic model of crime the costs for committing crimes decrease for the non-targeted group, so their offending will increase. In religiously motivated terrorism this substitution effect occurs as well in the form of converts who commit suicide attacks. Harcourt therefore comes to the conclusion that "(i)f we assume elasticity among rational actors, then profiling will increase offending among member(s) of the non-profiled group" (Harcourt 2006 : 18). Indeed, Harcourt gives names and examples of converts, who committed terrorist acts, which will be specified and completed later in this chapter. These examples may be considered as evidence of a substitution process in terrorism.

However, simply because the costs for committing e.g. a suicide attack (and the probability of being detected) decrease for a certain kind of people, these people do not necessarily increase their terrorist activity. One may assume that terrorists – especially religious terrorists, have motives to commit a suicide attack. These motives arise out of a specific biography, political understanding or worldview. Consequently their motives to commit a terrorist attack, often with deadly consequences for themselves, are very specific. This process cannot by implication be presumed for a non-targeted group that might not even have any religious or political background which prompts them to engage in terrorist activities. In other words: the 'white old lady' does not necessarily commit a terrorist attack because she is less likely to be detected. Yet, substitution effects in terrorism do exist and are – as it will be pointed out later in this chapter, on the rise. It is important to emphasize though that substitution effects on the 'actor-level' happen in the frameworks of a conscious ideological decision and the substitute actors' attacks are still religiously or politically motivated. The substitution effect therefore affects only the outer appearance of actors, not their ideology, which – again – suggests that not everyone of the non-targeted group may engage in terrorism.

Harcourt further argues that some substitution is inevitable. Therefore the central question is if substitution outweighs the benefits of profiling. To answer this question it is important to know if the targeted and the non-targeted group are indeed equally elastic to profiling as suggested by the economic model (s. earlier graph in 4.1 Theoretical foundation: Rational choice & target hardening). The assumption of equal elasticity may not be valid in real life. So the comparative elasticity of the two groups is what matters. If the offending of the targeted group is less elastic, meaning less responsive to profiling than other groups, "(…) then targeting them for enforcement efforts will increase the overall amount of crime in society because the increase in crime by members of the non-profiled group will exceed the decrease in crime by members of the profiled group" (Harcourt 2006 : 20). There is no a priori reason why the targeted group, here young Muslim men, should be less elastic to profiling than the non-targeted group. However, we do assume they have different offending rates, so why should their elasticity be the same? To evaluate the effectiveness of profiling it is therefore important to find out if young Muslim men are indeed less elastic to profiling than non-Muslim men and women. If members of the non-profiled group would engage in terrorism more easily when the costs decreased – it would be possible for terrorist organizations to recruit from outside of the profiled group. This would increase the amount of terrorism in the long term (Ibid. : 20). Mathematically, Harcourt describes the same effect for a similar phenomenon of ethnic profiling in drug trafficking, which can be applied to the terrorism context just as well.

In the following formula Er denotes the elasticity of each ethnic group (M denotes 'minority'/targeted group; W denotes 'whites'/non-targeted group). Or denotes the offending rate of each group. If EM is less than EW, we can denote the relationship in the following way:

$$x \, EM = EW, \text{ where } x > 1$$

If we assume that minority terrorists have lower elasticity by a factor of x, then ethnic profiling will decrease the profiled crime only if the following condition holds true:

$$OM > x \, OW$$

In other words, if minority terrorists (targeted group) have lower elasticity than white terrorists (non-targeted group), ethnic profiling will decrease the amount of profiled crime only if minority-terrorist offending is greater than white-terrorist offending times the elasticity differential x. If, for example white-terrorist elasticity is two times greater than minority-terrorist elasticity, then ethnic profiling will only reduce terrorist attacks if minority-terrorist offending is more than two times greater than white-terrorist offending (Harcourt 2007 : 125ff).

The following graph shows the instance of different substitutions in the targeted and non-targeted group: if the non-targeted group has a low internal group search rate and the targeted group has a high internal group search rate (ethnic profiling), but due to the targeted groups' low elasticity and substitution effects their offending rate is finally the same (as indicated at Time 2) and this offending rate, again, is achieved above the average offending rate at Time 1, profiling increases the overall amount of terrorist attacks.

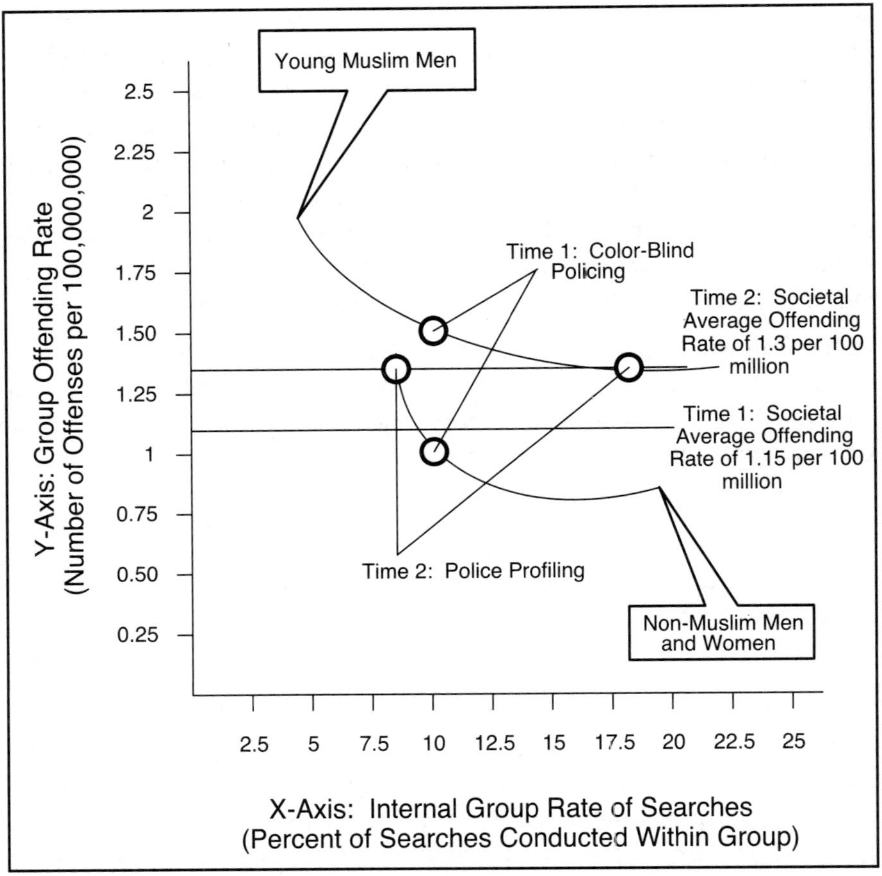

Fig. 6: A Model of Profiling with Different Elasticities (Harcourt 2007 : 21)

In fact, there is another premise that needs to be taken into account in Harcourt's model, provided that Harcourt's targeted group of 'young Muslim men' is profiled and selected for searches on the basis of their skin color, that is on the basis of actual ethnic profiling. Ethnic profiling is often employed in cases of religiously motivated terrorism, and as stated earlier, the conflation of race and religion leads to the assumption that race is an indicator for religion, but it does not necessarily have to be an indicator. So if members of the non-targeted group commit terrorist attacks for the reason that they are consciously 'deployed' by the radical Muslim community, the elasticity of young Muslim men as young Asian looking men may in fact be as high as the elasticity of the non-targeted, white men and women. Young Asian looking men would indeed commit less terrorist attacks, because but they would recruit from outside of the 'ethnic group' in order to not be detected themselves. In his model, Harcourt rather talks about the elasticity of the radical Muslim community in general, including Asian looking men and whites, which would have a low elasticity to profiling. This could of course be very likely. However, it would not be called ethnic profiling any longer, but profiling based on religion. However, if young Asian looking men still committed terrorist attacks (because their elasticity is low) and they recruited people from outside of the ethnic group, then the overall amount of terrorist attacks would be even higher. But this process would not be called substitution, but e.g. supplementary recruitment.

To answer these questions of different elasticities, Harcourt states, there is no empirical evidence. However in 1988 Jon Cauley and Eric Im explored the impact of the installation of metal detectors on different types of terrorist attacks to evaluate possible substitution effects on what will be called a 'strategic level'. With a permanent decrease of airplane hijackings, other types of terrorist attacks increased proportionally (Cauley/Im 1988 : 27ff). Walter Enders and Todd Sandler reach the same conclusion in their 1993 article on 'The Effectiveness of Antiterrorism Policies': mandatory Screening coincided with a sharp decrease in Skyjackings, but coincided with other kind of attacks, such as barricade missions and kidnappings. This was consistent with the assumption that

> "(…) terrorist groups substituted away from skyjackings and complementary events involving protected persons and into other kinds of hostage incidents. (…) The evidence seems to be that retaliatory raids induce terrorists to intertemporally substitute attacks planned for the future into the present to protest the retaliation. Within a relatively few quarters, terrorist attacks resumed the same mean number of events." (Enders/Sandler 1993 : 835)

According to Enders and Sandler, as well as Cauley and Im, the target hardening on US embassies resulted in a decrease of attacks against US interests, but in a substitute toward assassinations (Enders/Sandler 1993 : 842), and barricade and hostage taking events (Cauley/Im 1988 : 30). Enders and Sandler concluded that "(…) the unintended consequences of an antiterrorism policy may be far more costly than intended consequences, and must be anticipated" (Enders/Sandler 1993 : 843). Furthermore they explain in a latter publication that this kind of policy might lead to innovation effects, which aggravate the situation:

> "In the long term, terrorists will develop ingenious countermeasures to circumvent the technology. Immediately after airport vigilance was increased as a result of 9/11, Richard Reid (aka Tariq Rajah) was discovered on a flight from Paris to the United States with an explosive device in his shoes. Now that airport security routinely inspects shoes, plastic guns, electronic jamming equipment, bottles of flammable liquid or other explosive devices are predicted to be hidden on (or in) the terrorist or in carry-on luggage. Thus, there are dynamic strategic interactions; authorities must be vigilant to improve technology by anticipating ways of circumventing current technological barriers." (Enders/Sandler 2002/4 : 18)

These dynamic strategic interactions may be just as relevant for substitution effects on the actor-level, which are the main focus of this thesis. Although there seems to be very little evaluations of counter-terrorism strategies – substitution effects as well as the comparative elasticity of different groups – there is a remarkable amount of examples of substitution effects. In 2003, Judge Jean Louis Bruguière, who was the former French investigating magistrate in counter-terrorism affairs, stated that al Quaeda was developing a new focus on recruiting women and converts to Islam (Leiken 2004 : 107). The Dutch General Intelligence and Security Service (AIVD) and the British Home and Foreign Offices released studies on jihadi recruits' backgrounds in the following years. This shows a general development in Europe to focus on homegrown terrorism as a newer phenomenon. However, the problem is not easy to address and monitoring is not an option in consideration of civil liberties interests:

> "In September 2007, Günther Beckstein, the Bavarian minister of the interior, proposed registering and observing every convert to Islam in Germany in order to determine whether the future Muslim would pursue a liberal or an Islamist orientation. This suggestion provoked an uproar. Critics said it put converts under general suspicion, undercut religious dialogue, and contradicted the principle of religious freedom. Such populist tactics, though, are likely to be

> counterproductive. (…) Europeans would certainly argue that turning all converts to Islam into terrorism suspects runs counter to the ideals of European liberalism." (Uhlmann 2008 : 1f).

Furthermore, the terrorist profile is changing in a way that would make a focus on the traditional Muslim terrorist profile pointless. A study of al Quaeda terrorists conducted four years ago by Marc Sageman comprised social backgrounds, and the result is surprising: 90 percent came from a relatively stable background, upwardly and geographically mobile, speaking three to six languages and were sent abroad to study:

> "Three quarters were from middle-class or upper-class families, two thirds went to college and two thirds were professionals or semi-professionals, often engineers, physicians, architects or scientists. The average age for making an active commitment to violent jihad was 26, and three quarters of the terrorists were married, most of them with children. Only one in a hundred had shown any form of psychotic disorder. Two thirds became drawn towards a terror group while living in a country that was not their homeland." (Norfolk 2007 : 1)

According to Sageman there were three waves of global Salafi jihad with different actors: the first actors were companions of bin Laden in Aghanistan in the 1980s. The second wave consisted of the best and brightest of the Middle East, who became radicalized in the West. The third wave reflects the development toward homegrown terrorists, who are second and third generation immigrants in the West, less educated and with more criminal elements. The tendency toward waves of different recruits does not mean that the actors of the second or first waves are not active any longer (Ibid. : 2). The profiles of the same category of (jihadi) terrorism, changed through substitution effects, but the original actors are still active. These findings support the assumption by Harcourt described earlier: substitution effects may increase the overall amount of terrorism.

Furthermore, these findings suggest that substitution has two dimensions: firstly, substitution works as a conscious decision to substitute terrorist actors to avoid a certain profile and secondly, substitution is a rather self-evident social process due to migration, globalization and other social developments. Yet, the first scenario is relevant to the understanding of the effects of ethnic profiling.

Substitution does not only have two dimensions considering the different motivations or reasons for it, but it is furthermore put into practice on different levels. Substitution works on mainly three levels: it concerns terrorist strategies, techniques or instruments, and actors. Substitution of terrorist strategies is for example the shift from skyjacking to other kinds of transportation, such as trains as in the Madrid bombings or the public transport system in the London bombings. Substitution of terrorist strategies may also occur on a structural level, which has less to do with what the attack aims at, and more with the logistics of how the goal is achieved. This again is closely connected to instruments that are used to plan an attack. An example of the logistic kind of substitution is the shift away from terrorist group actors, as the 'Hamburg cell' of the 9/11 attacks, to lone attackers.

This is what is happening in Jerusalem. Even though the Palestine-Israel conflict is obviously no not modeled on European terrorist attacks and does not concern jihadi terrorism, it is still an example that should be taken into account, since it may be of general significance. After Ghassan Abu Tir, a worker on a construction site, attacked 16 people with a bulldozer, the police said that the "(…) attacker apparently acted on his own, underscoring what police said could be a series of attacks by 'lone attackers' in the short-term" (Lefkovits 2008 : 2). This incident is an example of the second kind of substitution, the substitution of terrorist techniques or instruments. The attacker did not use explosives to achieve a goal but substituted bombs with a bulldozer, probably because it would be less likely to be profiled or stopped and searched. The first bulldozer-attack happened on the 2nd of July 2008 when "(a) Palestinian man had driven a bulldozer into a bus and several cars in Jerusalem, killing three people, before being shot dead" (BBC NEWS 2008c : 1). The article continues with a statement on a shift away from suicide bombings: "Attacks by Palestinian militants in Jerusalem have been a rare occurrence in recent years, with none of their trademark suicide bombings since September 2004" (Ibid. : 2). The same happened again three weeks later when Ghassan Abu Tir "(…) rammed his construction vehicle into a city bus and several cars on a central thoroughfare in the capital (…), wounding 15 people before being shot dead by a Druse border police officer and a civilian passerby" (Lefkovits 2008 : 1).

The implications of ethnic profiling are the main focus of this thesis however. Therefore substitution on the actor-level is the most relevant kind of substitution, such as homegrown terrorism or the recruitment of converts. A well-known example of substitution in Germany refers to the already mentioned attack, which was planned by Germans in Oberschledorn in 2007. Two of them were converts: Fritz G. was at the time 28 years old, born in Munich, had studied industrial engineering and had converted to Islam at the age of 18. Daniel S. also had converted to Islam at the age of 18 and had lived as an Arabic- and Koran-student in Egypt for a couple of years. Only the 28-year old Turk Adem Y. matched the profile and had traveled to Pakistan for 'terrorist-instruction' (Wanzeck 2007 : 2f). Similar examples are known from the US, for instance John Walker Lindh, who was serving as a soldier for the Taliban (Ellman 2003 : 688) and Timothy Mc Veigh, who killed 168 people with the bombing of the Alfred P. Murrah Federal Building in Oklahoma City (BBC NEWS 2001c : 1). But terrorism suspects from atypical backgrounds are increasing in Western Europe, too:

> "(…) police across Europe are arresting significant numbers of women, teenagers, white-skinned suspects and people baptized as Christians – groups that in the past were considered among the least likely to embrace Islamic radicalism. The demographics of those being arrested are so diverse that many European counterterrorism officials and analysts say they have given up trying to predict what sorts of people are most likely to become terrorists. Age, sex, ethnicity, education and economic status have become more and more irrelevant." (Whitlock 2007 : 1)

More and more women are deployed for suicide attacks: Bouchra El-Hor, for example is a young Dutch Moroccan mother, who studied business in college. Muriel Degauque, a 38 year old blond white Catholic converted to Islam, who committed a suicide attack in November 2005 in Iraq. (Ibid. : 1f) Cossor Ali, a 24-year old mother, was suspected of smuggling liquid explosives onto a flight in her infant daughter's bottle. Dutch counterterrorism officials say that there is a significant rise in the number of female suspects. Edwin Bakker, a researcher at the Clingendael Institute of The Hague said that simple matters, such as the influence of some charismatic Moroccan boys on emotionally needy women, are not to be underestimated when it comes to manipulation and criminal acts of young Dutch women

(Whitlock 2007 : 2f)10. Already in 1986 a pregnant Irish woman aboard an Israel-bound flight got caught carrying a bomb in her luggage, which had been placed there without her knowledge by her Jordanian boyfriend (NY Times 1986 : 1).

Other factors that might lead converts to radicalization are for example that "(c)onverts wanting to explore and learn more about their new religion are often attracted to fundamentalist interpretations as they seek 'pure' and 'true' Islam" (Uhlmann 2008 : 3). Those who convert to Islam for practical purposes rarely become extremists. Others have a bigger chance of becoming radical:

> "Conversion is, in part, a migration from one worldview to another, described by sociologist Thomas Luckmann as a decision to go shopping in a supermarket of religious goods. As the individual tries to reconcile his old and new belief systems, he selects explanations that best meet his needs. Sometimes, this involves the endorsement of terrorism as a means of righting perceived wrongs." (Ibid. : 3)

Motives to convert are diverse. One reason could be the search for meaning and guidance, "(…) for example, by adherence to Shari'a (Islamic law), which provides rules that the convert believes are 'not arbitrary', like man-made laws" (Ibid. : 3). Furthermore the search for a higher purpose and the quest for social integration are important factors. The new religion can also be used as a means to articulate criticism of Western society, share the sense of alienation from the dominant culture, or to project sentiments of rebellion. The acquired religion allows the convert to express a new identity in everyday routines, such as in prayers (Ibid. : 3f).

All these findings lead to a categorization of substitution effects in terrorism, which could be visualized like this, here by means of prime examples:

---

[10] These examples were chosen to demonstrate new developments of substitution. It cannot be evaluated, how significant the influence of Moroccan boys on Dutch young women really is and to what extent this influences the development in general. The quoted examples could as well be singular events. It is not the author's intention to theoretically shift the responsibility for becoming radicalized from young European women to immigrants from the Middle East.

	Strategies	Instruments/ Techniques	Actors
Conscious Deployment	Shift from skyjackings to public transport system/shift from terrorist cells to lone attackers	Shift from solid bombs in luggage to liquid explosives, bulldozers	Shift from "young Asian looking men" to converts, women, children, teenagers, white-skinned ethnic groups
Social Processes	Shift from terrorist cells to lone attackers	-	vide supra/ Muslim radicals of the second or third generation in Europe

Fig. 7: Possibilities of Substitution Effects in Terrorism

Some examples could fit both categories – conscious deployment and social processes – such as the example of the lone attackers. Making use of lone attackers could be a consciously deployed technique to avoid being part of a terrorist cell or being monitored because of that. It could just as well be a result of what the Hamas say is a "(…) 'natural' response to 'a continued aggression against our people in the West Bank and Jerusalem'" (BBC NEWS 2008c : 2; similarly quoted in Lefkovits 2008 : 3).

From these statements one can conclude that profiling can lead to different kinds of political reactions to terrorism and to the profiled groups themselves. The profiled group may be subjects of integrative approaches, such as by the Jerusalem police chief Cmdr. Aharon Franco, who said at a police briefing after the bulldozer attack that "(…) it was wrong to blame all the Arab residents of east Jerusalem, noting that the attackers were the 'exceptions'" (Lefkovits 2008 : 2). Repressive approaches could lead to the following consequences for the targeted group: the demolishing of their homes, the deportations of the families, the revocation of their residency or background checks on construction site workers, as well as routine patrols of the sites, as suggested by some officials (Ibid. : 2f).

This example from the Israel-Palestine conflict indicates that profiling a certain group can lead to an aggravation of the situation. It might result in the repression of the targeted group. Furthermore, profiling could entail more and new ways to evade the profile by substitution. In this way the overall amount of attacks increase if the targeted group has a low elasticity, which it might very likely develop under circumstances of repression. Subsequently, new techniques, strategies or actors lead to more profiling and more security checks and therefore to even less liberty. This, again, spurs the targeted groups' impulse to innovation and new kinds of attacks. The repressive elements of counter-terrorism measures work as a catalyst or motor for the targeted group to develop low elasticity, because of the perceived injustice[11]. This is a possible repressive model of profiling:

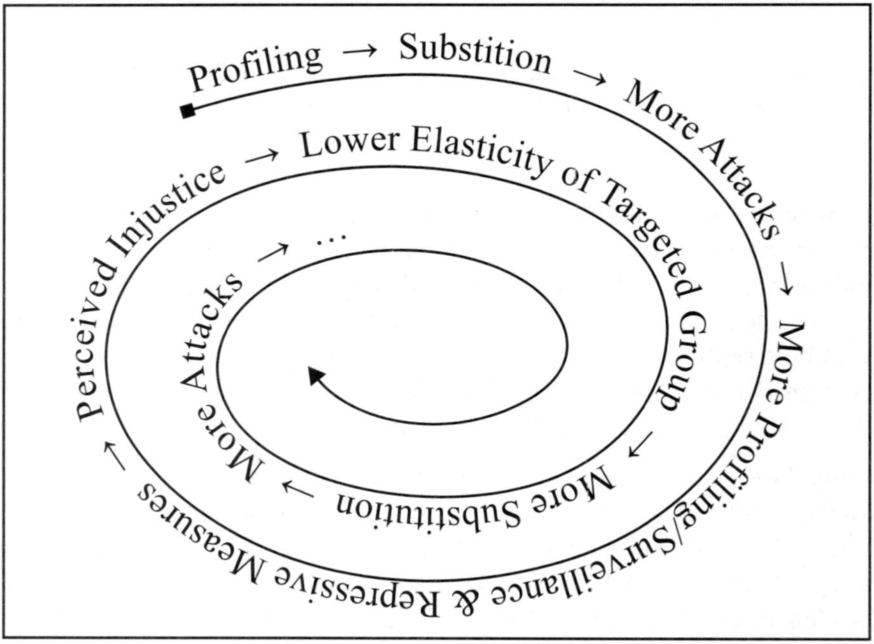

Fig. 8: Interdependency and Increase of Terrorism, Profiling and Repressive Counter-terrorism Measures

[11] These assumptions are supported in the model of the 'low trust globalization'. A low trust globalization is characterized by drastic controls and precautionary measures. It describes a world that is very legalistic, that is influenced by a 'coalition of the willing' (Rose 2006 : 51f). A typical actor or project of a low trust globalization could, for example, be the UK police with the campaign: 'If you suspect it, report it'. It urges citizens to report it to the police when they see people taking pictures of sensitive sites. (http://cms.met.police.uk/news/policy_organisational_news_and_general_information/partnerships/if_you_suspect_it_report_it)

Theoretical Conclusions on the Effectiveness of Ethnic Profiling

The central question is if ethnic profiling is effective, that is to say if it makes Europe safer. The benefits of ethnic profiling therefore have to outweigh the disadvantages. To answer this question, it makes sense to primarily call on the results achieved by ethnic profiling. The German dragnet investigation, for example, proved largely unsuccessful. The profiling parameters were widened so much that they were finally useless: 8.3 million individuals were analyzed, 32,000 persons were identified as potential 'sleepers' and yet no single person was charged with terrorism offenses. British Stop and Search under Terrorism Act 2000 in 2003/4 had a success rate of 0.06%: 8,120 people were stopped, five were arrested and all of the arrested persons were white (Moeckli 2006 : 17). This reflects what Vincent Cannistraro, former head of counter-terrorism at the CIA stated, namely that he doesn't know of "(…) any example where profiling caught a terrorist" (Zakaria 2002 : 6). Yet, important arrests have been made across Europe, for example in Perugia, after Italian police raided a mosque (s. Chapter 3.3). As a result, the region is safer. However, in the aftermath of 9/11 more than 600 people were arrested in the UK, 100 were charged with terrorism offenses and 15 people have been convicted of such crimes. Of those 15 convicted people approximately three were Muslim (OSI 2007 : 19). This, again, emphasizes the disproportion of these measures.

It is obvious that there are collateral benefits in connection with ethnic profiling in counter-terrorism, such as immigration enforcement outcomes. A prime example of these mutual benefits is the mass identity checks (s. Chapter 3.2).

Moreover, the UK Anti-Terrorism, Crime and Security Act (ATCSA) 2001 can be consulted for immigration detention reasons and was used against Muslim men from Middle Eastern and North African States (Knight 2005 : 1). Germany has a strict policy of deportations in counter-terrorism, too, mainly targeted at 'Islamist extremists' and 'dangerous Islamists', such as the imam of the Frankfurt mosque, Said Khobaib Sadat[12] and the 'caliph of Cologne', Metin Kaplan[13], who have already been deported. This shows

---

12 Verwaltungsgericht Frankfurt am Main, decision of 26 January 2006, case no 5 E 5870/04.A

13 Oberverwaltungsgericht Münster, decision of 26 May 2004, case no 8 A

that not just anti-terrorism measures are used for immigration detention, but similarly immigration laws are used for antiterrorism purposes, too.

Another collateral benefit of anti-terrorism measures is deterrence. Raids and mass identity controls are intentionally accomplished not primarily to uncover terrorist activities, but to deter them (OSI 2007 : 17ff). Alain Chouet, former head of France's external-intelligence agency told Le Figaro: "One cannot quite imagine Anglo-Saxon countries imitating our tactic of harassment, sometimes without real elements of proof. (…) Sometimes it's a bit borderline, but it upsets the networks, prevents them from taking action" (Ibid. : 17ff). However, these police actions equate a large number of peaceful Muslims with potential terrorists (over- inclusion). In a similar manner, anti-radicalization-techniques large numbers of young Muslims with a very small group of individuals, who might engage in terrorist activities (Ibid. : 18).

All these collateral benefits may on the one hand be useful, but it is questionable whether they make Europe safer in the end. Finally, it is very likely that the following disadvantages and methodological breaches of ethnic profiling in counterterrorism outweigh the mentioned benefits: firstly, to implement it strategically, ethnic profiling often involves enormous financial resources for staff and equipment and is, moreover, time-consuming. Other kinds of crime reduction efforts may therefore be neglected and the general crime rate might rise. This was, for example, the case in the German dragnet investigation (Moeckli 2006 : 17). Ethnic profiling also shifts the officials' attention away from behavioral aspects, which could be more promising and sustainable in the counterterrorism context. Behavioral profiling will be discussed as an alternative in the conclusion of this thesis. Secondly, because of over- and under-inclusion ethnic profiling has a huge margin of error. Incidentally, one reason that could explain over-inclusion is simply the visibility of ethnicity. Findings in social psychology indicate that ethnicity could be over-emphasized in profiling because of its conspicuousness, and therefore possibly distorts the process (OSI 2007 : 16). Thirdly, the fact that ethnic profiling rarely produces concrete results underscores its ineffectiveness. Finally, ethnic profiling might in fact aggravate the situation by substitution effects and increase the minority

---

3852/03.A; Verwaltungsgericht Köln, decision of 12 October 2004, case no 12 L 1418/04

communities' sense of isolation. Maleiha Malik, lecturer at the Kings College, London, who focuses on anti-discrimination law regarding religious minorities and Muslim women, supports the theory that social isolation and alienation of minorities will multiply the enemy (Tigner 2007 : 2). The process of alienation and its possible repercussions on security policy are reconsidered in the next chapter.

4.3 The Social Aftermath of Ethnic Profiling and Repercussions on Security Policy

Ethnic profiling is likely to involve humiliation, which leads to alienation. These secondary effects may in the long run backfire on security policy. The cause-and-effect-chain commences on the individual level with the singled-out person. Ethnic profiling impinges on the individual's rights of freedom from unfair arrest and detention, freedom of religion, freedom from interference in one's private and family life, freedom of movement and freedom of association, and therefore legitimizes discrimination (OSI 2007 : 19), which will be discussed in chapter five. Ethnic profiling thereby causes profound emotional costs for the individual, especially if singled out innocently. Being stopped and searched on the basis of ethnic profiling causes a feeling of being intimidated, degraded or humiliated by law enforcement officials, more than neutral law enforcement measures do (Kennedy 1997 : 157ff).

These individual experiences are, as Moeckli argues, likely to be translated into group effects: individuals are singled out because they match a set of group characteristics. This leads to the assumption that the whole group is inherently suspect, which stigmatizes and victimizes entire communities (Moeckli 2006 : 19). Some authors even refer to this process as 'racializing crime' or 'criminalizing race' (Leadership conference on Civil Rights Education Fund 2003 : 19). As pointed out in the last chapters, a vast majority of the targeted group is innocently victimized with such procedures, which will in turn result in alienation. The UK Police Chief Superintendent Ali Dizaei reminded the public that the Muslim community is not only a secondary victim of the London bombings because they are being alienated, but were also primary victims, who died in the attack. Whereas Haras Rafiq, spokesman for the Sufi Muslim council favored such screening measures, if they were carried out professionally. However, Inayat

Bunglawala, spokesman for the Muslim council of Britain supported the policeman's warning: "There is concern that such profiling would perhaps only contribute to further alienating a group whose close co-operation is essential in countering terror" (Chorley/Linden 2006 : 1). Bunglawala mentions the negative implications the alienation of Muslims may have for law enforcement efforts: mistrust – which is especially disadvantageous in the terrorism-context. The cooperation of the screened communities could be a precious source of information for the police, if 'sleepers' were indeed Muslim, as the government claims. Thus, the opposite is the case: ethnic profiling increases the level of distrust and ethnic tensions between the police and Muslims.

It is problematic that these alienating procedures are furthermore experienced as state power, which undermines the confidence of the Muslim community in the rule of law (Moeckli 2006 : 20). The alienating effect is all the more disastrous considering that the second and third generation Muslims are already feeling dislocated from society. According to Clive Walker, a terrorism specialist and professor of Criminal Justice at Leeds University, young men of the 'in-between generation' are particularly susceptive to radical Islam:

> "It's a kind of in-between state, a symptom of rejection in many ways. They feel rejected, but equally they reject the available cultures, both of their fathers and of the society they find themselves in (…) So they're looking for some kind of explanation or some kind of cultural philosophy which makes them feel important and valued in ways which they don't find from the other two obvious sources of cultural expression." (Norfolk 2007 : 2)

Some of the large-scale operations targeting Muslim communities gain a lot of media-attention. Some authors assume that these well-covered operations contribute to fostering public stereotypes associating Muslims with potential terrorists. Consequently, law-enforcement officials benefit from this media attention, since they can "(…) send the message to the public that 'the enemies' are being watched and weeded out of society" (OSI 2007 : 19f). Therefore, the negative stereotype is perceived and fostered throughout the whole society. Prejudices grow, which may result in growing tensions between the racial groups: targeted minorities and non-targeted whites.

Another social cost can be described with what Harcourt calls the ratchet effect. The ratchet is a distortion that "(…) occurs when successful profiling produces a supervised population that is disproportionate to the distribution of offending by racial group" (Harcourt 2007 : 28). This is a version of over-inclusion which mainly ends up with incarceration. Harcourt described this model for the example of ethnic profiling in drug dealing offenses, but it is possible to translate the model into one model of ethnic profiling in counter-terrorism. However, the there are less people involved in terrorist activities and being incarcerated for terrorism offenses than there are being incarcerated for drug dealing or other average offenses. Terrorism is, for example, not listed as a category in the British Crime Survey and Police Recorded Crime 2007/2008[14]. Its offending rate is too low to be comparable to other offending rates. So are the detention rates. Therefore the ratchet effect, which mainly explains after-effects of imprisonment, will not be introduced in detail here. But its main features will be mentioned to demonstrate the disproportionate distribution of criminal justice contacts of the profiled group. The ratchet effect is furthermore interesting in this context, because the subsequent effects of social exclusion are the same: it is likely that individuals, who were searched or arrested under the Terrorism Act, often suffer similar consequences to those, who were incarcerated.

Let us assume that the majority population has an average offending rate in terrorism and a minority group has a slightly above average offending rate in terrorism. If the police search randomly, the result will reflect the offending rates: the percentage of the minority in the overall distribution of terrorist offenders is, due to its slightly higher offending rate, higher than its share of the general distribution in the population. If the police now takes this as a reason to profile more people of the higher-offending group, the police will simply find more offenders in the higher-offending group and incarcerate more people of the higher-offending group: "This is precisely the distortion created by using actuarial methods. It is what begins the ratchet" (Harcourt 2007 : 152). Now, if the police then rely on the statistics which resulted from their own profiling and therefore reflects

---

[14] For further information see: http://www.homeoffice.gov.uk/rds/pdfs08/hosb0708.pdf

the actual breakdown of the offending population, they will likely engage in more profiling of the high-offending minority group. The distortion increases (Ibid. : 155). In principle, this may be continued until all the offenders of the high-offending minority group are incapacitated, but the offenders of the majority group are completely underrepresented in the incapacitated group. Profiling then works as a self-confirming prophecy. If we now assume minority-group profiling is done partly because of the group's ethnicity and 'visibility', in this case being a young man of Middle Eastern appearance, ethnic profiling leads to a disproportionate distribution of minority-group offenders with law enforcement contacts.

The ratchet effect would also work under conditions of elasticity. "The extent of the ratchet, in fact, will depend on the amount of elasticity within each group and on the relative offending rate" (Ibid. : 157), but the effect would still appear. Furthermore,

> "(c)riminal profiling would also create a ratchet under those conditions: the same result, namely, increased disproportionality in the balance of the incarcerated population, would obtain if all groups had the same offending rate, but we allocated slightly more of our law enforcement resources to one minority group than their representation in the general population would warrant." (Harcourt 2007 : 156)

However, in the case of terrorism, these findings have to be considered under a specific condition: law enforcement officers often act on the assumption that there is no other offending group beside the minority offending group (s. chapter 4.1). This of course explains the amount of law enforcement effort devoted to find terrorists in Muslim communities. It is almost not appropriate to talk about a ratchet in the case of terrorism, because the disproportionate distribution of searches is already extremely high and there is almost no comparison group. It is therefore imperative to research more into substitution effects and different, or new kinds of terrorism to get to know more about offenders.

Finally, Harcourt explains that the social costs of the ratchet effect are the ultimate problem, as incarcerated individuals are often exposed to considerable secondary implications in terms of education, employment, and family lives: "Disproportionate criminal supervision and incarceration reduces work opportunities, breaks down families and communities, and disrupts education" (Harcourt 2007 : 161). These implications have already been mentioned and typified for wrongful arrests in counter-terrorism (chapter 4.2 on over-inclusion). It shall not be discussed here what the effects of incapacitation are, however – it is clear that there are some – which may lead to social deprivation and criminal activities.

Yet, it is obvious that not all wrongful arrests and searches made in counter-terrorism end up in incapacitation, but being searched or arrested under Terrorism Act already entail comparable implications, especially with the almost irreversible stigma of being a potential 'terrorist': unemployment, fewer educational opportunities, deepening poverty, loss of societal status and disruptions in Muslim communities.

The negative impact that the ratchet effect may have on communities can be visualized in a simple model developed by Harcourt, which is just as true for the terrorism context as it is for drug-related crime (on the basis of Harcourt 2007 : 163):

Police conduct →	**Social meaning** →	**Social norm** →	**Impact on community**
Racial profiling that produces a ratchet effect on the carceral population.	Muslims are suspect, require police supervision and are entitled to fewer liberties.	Presumed Muslim criminality.	Muslims are perceived as criminals and experience more discrimination.

Fig. 9: Negative Impact of the Ratchet Effect on Muslim Communities

Now, one assumption of this work is that the negative impact on the Muslim community caused by ethnic profiling might backfire on security policy with increased numbers of terrorist attacks (or a risen level of delinquency). This thesis draws upon two classical criminological theories to support and expand the findings described above: the general theory of strain caused by social inequality, and the defiance theory. Defiance theory focuses on possible delinquent reactions to procedural injustice, here caused by ethnic profiling. The general theory of strain explains possible delinquent reactions to the status of persistent discrimination or social inequality caused by the ratchet effect. Both theories are consulted to emphasize how ethnic profiling and its repercussions may backfire on security policy in the long run.

Discrimination, Social Inequality and the General Theory of Strain

> "Almost all of the revolutions which have changed the aspect of nations have been made to consolidate or to destroy social inequality" (Tocqueville 1961 : 302). Economic disparity and relative deprivation appear in less developed countries as well as in developed countries and are factors considered conducive to terrorism. This means that the mobilization of aggression depends on the social, economic and political circumstances of a society (Tocqueville 1961). This cause-and-effect-chain was on micro-level-for example, summarized in the frustration-aggression-hypothesis, and the same coherences were later established for the macro-level, too (Wiberg 1990). Social inequality and armed conflict were also found to correlate positively (Boswell/Dixon 1990): the extent to which social inequality or relative deprivation appears- defines the probability of armed conflict or terrorism[15].

However, ethnic profiling per se does not cause relative deprivation, but ethnic profiling might, as described above, stigmatize and frustrate a whole community, since singular experiences are translated into group effects. Therefore, it might produce aggravated social conditions as a secondary effect, for example: the stigma that Muslims are likely to be involved in terrorist activities debars them from getting a job.

The case of Lofti Raissi, the already mentioned case of a pilot who was wrongfully accused for having been part of the 9/11 attacks and impris-

---

[15] Jan Oskar Engene describes how relative deprivation is closely connected to the legitimacy of the state: the three most important challenges that the state needs to overcome to prove its legitimacy are a) unmet ethnic requirements, b) problems in continuity while establishing democracy, c) problems of integration of political fringe groups. He finally comes to the conclusion that integration problems and ideological terrorism correlate with each other (Engene 1998). This finding underscores the assumption of this work, namely that ethnic profiling in counterterrorism and its repercussions might lead to failed integration and a rise of Islamist terrorism.

oned for several months, shows that the label[16] of being a terrorist had a determining impact on his career and reputation. Lord justice Hooper stated while giving the judgment:

> "The public labelling of the appellant as a terrorist by the authorities in this country, and particularly by the [Crown Prosecution Service, the government's criminal prosecutors in England and Wales], over a period of many months has had and continues to have, so it is said, a devastating effect on his life and on his health. (...) He considers that, unless he receives a public acknowledgement that he is not a terrorist, he will be unable to get his life back together again." (Bright 2008 : 1)

Robert Agnew (1999) argues that these kinds of social conditions, or more generally put, social inequalities, produce strain. On a more abstract level, sources of strain could be the failure to achieve positively valued goals, like money, status, respect, and being treated in a nondiscriminatory manner. Goal blockage is one way how a loss of positive stimuli and the presentation of negative stimuli are produced. The growing amount of negative stimuli cause strain, which does not always result in crime, but creates a basis for delinquency:

> "Goal blockage, relative deprivation, and exposure to aversive stimuli increase the likelihood that community residents will experience a range of negative emotions, including anger and frustration. Aggregated levels of anger/frustration should have a direct effect on crime rates (…) These community characteristics not only produce angry/frustrated individuals but also increase the likelihood that such individuals will interact with one another. This further increases the level of strain/anger in the community" (Agnew 1999 : 127)

[16] The labeling approach could be another attempt to explain possible negative repercussions of ethnic profiling, which will not be discussed in detail in this thesis. The label 'potential terrorist' determines other peoples' perception of the criminalized person, and finally, the labeled person's self-definition. Eventually, the labeled individual will behave in accordance with his 'Master Status' (Becker 1963). However, 'terrorist' is an 'extreme' label and therefore it is questionable if such a self-definition would lead a person to commit homicide, for example. Thus, if the label would be 'outsider', because he could be a potential terrorist, it would be more probable that the individual lives up to this definition.

This theory emphasizes the assumption that the discriminatory practice of ethnic profiling has a negative influence on the community. Agnew later refers to ethnic discrimination as a violation of the desire to be treated in a fair manner, which therefore constitutes a distinct source of strain (Ibid. : 133). In this special case, it is very likely that the angry/frustrated individuals do not 'mistreat each other', as Agnew assumed earlier (Ibid. : 127), but rather act as a group: they have a 'common enemy', the law enforcement officials, who are considered the discriminating aggressor. Especially when it comes to discrimination based on ethnicity, it is more likely that the ethnical group discriminated against, in case they represent a minority (Muslims in Europe), gets into conflicts with the aggressor – not with each other. Agnew writes that "(n)egative experiences with the police (…) may generate feelings of injustice and increase the likelihood of further crime" (Ibid. : 133).

Agnew also states that "(c)riminal victimization is, in fact, one of the most serious types of strain to which individuals are subject, and data suggest that it is a major source of subsequent crime" (Ibid. : 128). The discrimination and victimization individuals experience through ethnic profiling, however, is experienced as power by the state. This fact skews the proportion of the parties in conflict: a Muslim minority struggles against representatives of the state. This might result in even more negative stimuli. The visibility of advantaged others, for example non-targeted whites, could lead to even more frustration.

Coping with this kind of strain could, amongst other things, result in radicalization and terrorist activities, as an aligned expression of frustration. These scenarios possibly hold true for societies in which ethnic profiling and other repressive measures of security policy are already advanced or the secondary effects of ethnic profiling are very strong, for example in Israel (s. bulldozer attack). An ethnic conflict of this degree has not yet been reached in Europe.

However, if ethnic profiling contributes to a rising level of strain in Muslim communities, it is very likely to contribute to the growth of the general crime rate in these communities, which is probably something that was not intended by the police. Nor is the widened gap between the police and the Muslim community a desired outcome.

Defiance Theory and Discriminatory Counter-Terrorism Measures

Defiance theory is another approach that brings possible negative repercussions of ethnic profiling on security policy into focus. Surprisingly, it has not been discussed in this exact context yet, although it constitutes a conclusive approach to the discriminatory aspect of ethnic profiling. However, defiance theory is developed to explain offenders' reactions, but in most cases of singled-out Muslims no offense actually happened, as described in chapter 4.2 on over-inclusion. Therefore, this thesis argues with defiance theory's terminology and mode of operation, but it does not presuppose a criminal act.

According to Sherman (1993) defiance may occur when four conditions are met:

> "1. The offender defines a criminal sanction as unfair. 2. The offender is poorly bonded to or alienated from the sanctioning agent or the community the agent represents. 3. The offender defines the sanction as stigmatizing and rejecting a person, not a lawbreaking act. 4. The offender denies or refuses to acknowledge the shame the sanction has actually caused him to suffer." (Sherman 1993 : 460).

With the preceding chapters' argumentation, these conditions are very likely to be met in the case of ethnic profiling, except that being singled out, stopped or searched is – as a general rule – not based on any offense or other evidence, as already stated. However, this emphasizes point three (sanction is stigmatizing) all the more. So the four conditions are generally met: the profiled individual defines the singling out as unfair (1). Law enforcement officials are representatives of the state that a lot of Muslims may indeed live in, but as stated earlier, they often identify more with the culture of their country of origin, or in the case of second and third generation immigrants, with neither their parents' cultural background nor that of the majority population. Therefore, the sanctioning agent represents a community that Muslims are not necessarily closely bonded to (2). Since for most of the singled out Muslims no lawbreaking act actually happened, it would be a normal reaction to define the sanction or police action against them as stigmatizing (3). Because of (3), the offender probably refuses to acknowledge the fact that he is under suspicion.

Sherman's defiance theory further says that sanctions are defined as unfair if one of the two following conditions is met:

> "1. The sanctioning agent behaves with disrespect for the offender, or for the group to which the offender belongs, regardless of how fair the sanction is on substantive grounds. 2. The sanction is substantively arbitrary, discriminatory, excessive, undeserved, or otherwise objectively unjust." (Ibid. : 461)

The discriminatory element of ethnic profiling is, as exposed in chapter 4.2, part of the methodology, because ethnicity is used as a basis for singling-out individuals, and therefore its implications are similarly discriminating or 'undeserved', as Sherman puts it in condition number two. So the 'sanction' or law enforcement act, which in this case means being stopped and searched or put under wrongful arrest, is unjust. It is very likely that even if a Muslim person was stopped and searched for a reason, the underlying technique, by which means the individual was singled out, is defined as unfair.

According to Sherman, there are three reactions to unfair treatment by law enforcement: 1. If the poorly bonded person accepts the shame that a stigmatizing law enforcement act provokes, the act will be irrelevant or have a deterrent effect to future offending. 2. If a well-bonded person defines the act as unfair, the unfairness may weaken the deterrent effect and make it irrelevant to future conduct. "But even if the offender (…) denies the shame, proud defiance is unlikely because it is less valued than pride associated with social bonds" (Ibid. : 461). 3. If poorly bonded persons deny the shame they feel and respond with rage, the unfair stigmatizing act will increase their future rates of offending.

Sherman defines the subsequent process like this:

> "This unacknowledged shame leads to an emotion of angry pride at defying the punishment. That pride predisposes the defiant offender to repeat the sanctioned conduct, symbolically labeling the sanctions or sanctioners, and not the offender's own acts as truly shameful and morally deserving of punishment. In the process, the victims or targets of the sanctioned acts become vicarious substitutes for the state or its sanctioning representatives." (Ibid. : 461).

However, as argued earlier, in the case of ethnic profiling, the individual did not necessarily commit an offense, which it can 'repeat to symbolically label the sanctioners as truly shameful'. It is, however, imaginable that the repercussions could function in a similar manner: the ongoing labeling and discrimination leads to a defiance reaction, which either makes the wrongfully sanctioned person become more radical and get involved in exactly the kind of crime that he was stopped and searched- or wrongfully arrested for. This assumption would be underscored by the labeling approach. Or the angry pride leads to the assumption that the sanctioners' wrongful conduct needs to be punished instead, as described by Sherman, except in this case the sanctioners' conduct is indeed wrongful. So the singled-out person or group would start to act more radically against the sanctioners or against substitutes representing the sanctioners. This act of revolt could, in the worst case, be realized with illegal means and involve violence, such as terrorist attacks or other kinds of crime. There is at least a high probability that the ongoing singling-out of Muslims has a negative effect on the Muslim community, which could involve some sort of defiant reaction by radical Muslims. This coherence will be later discussed by means of a deterrence-defiance model developed by John Braithwaite.

Sherman describes different kinds of defiance reactions: specific or individual defiance is the reaction of one person and the person's own sanction. General defiance is a reaction by a group or collective. There could be a collective reaction even if only a couple of members of that collective were singled out. Direct defiance is crime committed against the discriminating agent (aggressor) and indirect defiance is targeted at an institution or group representing the aggressor (Ibid. : 459). Specific defiance by a singled-out Muslim is likely, however general defiance in combination with indirect defiance is even more probable, because the coherence of a minority group that is discriminated against is likely to be high. The feeling of being alienated as a group, if a couple of members of the minority group are profiled, is very likely. Furthermore, ethnic profiling contributes to the ascription of 'potential terrorist' to the whole minority group. The possibility of being singled out rises for members of the minority group, therefore the coherence of the group will be even higher. Especially in cases where discrimination is involved, it is more of a risk to commit defiance as a single person directly against the aggressor, who is very likely to be more powerful, because he is a representative of the state (as, for example a police officer).

John Braithwaite draws upon Brehm and Brehm's (1981) theory of psychological reactance, which is a psychological model of deterrence and defiance. It says that when a threat is escalated, a deterrence curve with a positive slope, as well as a reactance or defiance curve with a negative slope occur. "Escalating threat simultaneously delivers more deterrence and more defiance (…). Whether deterrence 'works' depends on the positive slope of the deterrence curve being steeper than the negative slope of the defiance curve. The net effect of escalating threat is formally the sum of the two curves." (Braithwaite 2005 : 97)

The deterrence curve is stronger, if the freedom that is supposed to be regulated is not important to the people. Then the deterrence curve works as the rational choice theory predicts. However, if the freedom is important to the people, defiance reactions grow as a result. In the context of counter-terrorism, measures are based on deterrence. If a specific deterrence policy hurts a freedom which is important to the Muslim world, it simply provokes defiant reactions and "(…) continues cycles of tit-for-tat terror" (Ibid. : 97). Combining Sherman's findings with those of psychological reactance, we come to the same conclusion as Braithwaite: "(…) deterrence effects will exceed defiance effects when sanctions are seen as an outcome of fair procedures"(Ibid. : 97). According to Braithwaite, however, this assumption of procedural justice concerns more influential large-scale contexts than the implementation of ethnic profiling, such as choosing more peaceful counter-terrorism strategies before bombing Afghanistan. However, this procedural justice model still holds true for the ethnic profiling context on a smaller scale, just as Yahya Birt, a commissioning editor at a Muslim publisher's in Britain, writes: "(…) discriminatory treatment feeds the sort of alienation terrorist recruiters like to exploit" (Birt 2008 : 2). The question is therefore, how the targeted Muslim population perceives the exertion of ethnic profiling.

Furthermore, it is very likely that ethnic profiling and its media coverage do trigger a reciprocal reaction: on the one hand ethnic profiling produces a sense of fear of the police in the Muslim community. On the other hand it nurtures what may be called 'Islamophobia' in the European non-targeted white population. A 2004 survey by the Forum Against Islamophobia and Racism found that 80 percent of Muslims had been subjected to Islamophobia, 68 percent reported that they were treated differently and 32 percent of Muslims report being discriminated against at UK airports (FAIR 2004 : 22). According to a 2005 Home Office survey 5 percent of British Muslims had been stopped and searched by police, 42 percent felt they had been subject to suspicion and 44 percent of Muslims had experienced unfair treatment in the labor market, believing it to be due to their religion (Kitchen/Michaelson/ Wood 2005 : 21ff). In the same context the Open Society Institute concluded that

> "(…) equally damaging is the deep sense of fear that the use of profiling in counter-terrorist action has instilled among members of Muslim communities. (…) One of the most serious impacts of ethnic profiling is its contribution to stigmatizing members of targeted ethnic, religious or national groups. When the authorities single out members of certain groups for control and surveillance, and particularly when these actions are broadcast to the media, the message is sent that the entire ethnic or religious group presents a danger to society. Negative stereotypes are fostered and reinforced, contributing to existing social and political tendencies toward racism and xenophobia." (OSI 2007 : 20)

Closely connected to the media coverage is the reaction by the non-targeted white public as other surveys show. The reactions change with the time: in the direct aftermath of an attack and associated media coverage, fear and frustration apparently drive the non-targeted people to claim stricter sanctions and security measures. After a while this feeling of fear and frustration disappears and the opinions on security measures for the targeted group become more liberal again.

> "Surveys conducted in September 2001 found tolerance bending under the emotional strain of the attacks. Several questions show the public's fear and frustration right after the trade center attack, with 58 percent saying Arabs should undergo special security checks before boarding planes and 49 percent saying they should carry special identification (…) In January 2002, Public Agenda researchers found two-thirds of Americans agreed that racial pro-

> filing of Middle Easterners by law enforcement is 'understandable, but you wish it didn't happen'." (Bittle/Johnson 2002 : 1)[17]

A 2004 US Minority Rights and Relations Poll found that 40 percent of Non-Hispanic whites, 48 percent of Blacks and 54 percent of Hispanics thought that Racial Profiling on security checkpoints at airports was widespread, but altogether 53 percent said it was never justified (Carlson 2004 : 3).

---

[17] Although this example is taken from the USA, they are consulted to show the possible effect on Muslims through media coverage after an attack.

5. ETHNIC PROFILING IN EUROPEAN COUNTER-TERRORISM – LEGAL CONSIDERATIONS

Since terrorism is considered a highly dangerous crime with huge impacts and fatal consequences, anti-terrorism powers have –as a general rule – a wide scope of application. Law-enforcement authorities have far-reaching powers and enjoy wide discretion. Laws criminalizing the support of terrorism are broadly drafted, such as the British Terrorism Act 2006, Section 1, paragraph one, which establishes minimal actus reus and mens rea (objective and subjective matter of fact) requirements. The broader a law is drafted, the higher is the possibility of law enforcement officers to find a reason to investigate. Furthermore, judicial review, namely the supervision of public authorities in their exercise of power, is rarely accomplished (in the US it is even forbidden in some cases) which again leads to law enforcement officers having even less to defend their decisions before court. This authorization of law enforcement officers with appropriate laws is justified with the exclusive expertise that officers have in that field (Moeckli 2006: 3f).

These circumstances have a big impact on the conduct of law enforcement officers and the use of ethnic profiling. The European Counter-Terrorism Strategy regulates both, the integration and support of Muslim communities, as well as an implementation of counter-terrorism measures in a democratic way. However, it also creates a wide leeway concerning the gathering and exchange of data, as well as the conduct of identity checks at sensitive sites. The European Counter-Terrorism Strategy does not imply a paragraph explicitly on the use of ethnic profiling.

5.1 European Counter-Terrorism

In November 2004 the European Council announced the European Union's strategy for enhancing security over a five-year period: The Hague Program for Freedom, Justice and Security. It concentrates on illegal migration, terrorism and organized crime, and formulates concrete objectives such as the regulation of migration flows, control of the external borders of the Union, the fight against organized cross-border crime, repression of the threat of terrorism, realization of the potential cross-border police agencies and the increase of co-operation in criminal and civil matters (EC 2005 :

1). Concerning the fight against terrorism, the Hague Program focuses on prevention, preparedness and response. It includes the reduction of access to financial resources by terrorists, the exchange of information relevant to the investigation on terrorist activities and the protection of critical infrastructure. This entails two further projects: a Critical Infrastructure Warning Network (CIWIN) in 2005 and a pilot project for the victims of terrorist attacks in 2006.

The European Union Counter-Terrorism Strategy

One year after the Hague Program, the Council of the European Union proposed the European Union Counter-Terrorism Strategy, including a detailed action plan[1] with the crucial points of the Hague Program. In accordance with the Hague Program, the plan follows four strands of work: preventing, protecting, pursuing and responding. All of them follow the head note: "To combat terrorism while respecting human rights, and make Europe safer, allowing its citizens to live in an area of freedom, security and justice" (European Council Document 14469/04/05 REV 4: 6). Key elements are:

> "To prevent people turning to terrorism by tackling the factors or root causes which can lead to radicalization and recruitment, in Europe and internationally; To protect citizens and infrastructure (…) through improved security of borders, transport, and critical infrastructure; To pursue and investigate terrorists globally; to impede planning, travel, and communications; to disrupt support networks; to cut off funding and access to attack materials, and bring terrorists to justice; To (…) minimise the consequences of a terrorist attack, by improving capabilities to deal with: the aftermath; the co-ordination of the response; and the needs of the victims" (Ibid. : 3)

Implementing these objectives and promoting international standards for countering terrorism involves the collection, analysis and the sharing of information. The participating parties are EU bodies, as Europol, Eurojust, Frontex, and the United Nations as well as international organizations and key third countries (e.g. the USA). The European Commission provides a framework to help co-ordinate national policies. The responsibility

---

[1] The detailed action plan is according to the EU Counter-Terrorism Strategy paper reviewed every six months (Council of the European Union 2005 : 17).

however, lies primarily with the member states, which are also requested to focus on combating terrorism on a regional and local level.

The European Union Counter-Terrorism Strategy mentions different measures based on the integration and support of Muslim communities to tackle the root cause for terrorism. So the paper suggests the promotion of good governance, human rights, democracy, education and economic prosperity as well as the engagement in conflict resolution and fighting discrimination. However, the plan also places a strong emphasis on the surveillance of location, media and action that could be used for terrorist activities. The approach of these points is based on the exclusion of potential terrorists, rather than on anti-radicalization by means of integration. The paper suggests measures that could easily lead to scenarios described in chapter three – if the EU does not "(…) pursue its goals in a democratic and accountable way" (Ibid. : 3): "Given that the current terrorist threat has roots (…) beyond the EU" (Ibid. : 7), point 5 suggest a co-operation with third countries including ones of North Africa, the Middle East and South East Asia. Comparing the selection of the three areas to the examples of disproportionate ID checks or the screening of people from these three areas which were mentioned in chapter three, it can be assumed that the suggestions made in the EU plan had also unwanted effects. Similarly, paragraphs 9 and 17 suggest the monitoring of travel to conflict zones and the raise of standards in transport security. Paragraph 13 envisions to "(a)ddress incitement and recruitment in particular in key environments, for example prisons, places of religious training or worship (…)" (Ibid. : 9) and paragraph 16 proposes the "(…) capture and exchange of passenger data, and the inclusion of biometric information in identity and travel documents" (Ibid. : 10). This could lead to the denial of access to the Schengen area.

In addition to that, the paper puts forward a) the provision of necessary tools to collect intelligence, b) a risk analysis of the data gathered in the Visa Information System (VIS) conducted by Frontex, c) the exchange of information on terrorists[2], d) the availability of law enforcement information

2 On the occasion of a conference on 'New Alliances against Crime and Violence' held by the Federal Criminal Police Office in November 2005, the Minister of the Interior at the time Otto Schily referred to the 'Prümer agreement' from May 2005, which already scheduled an improvement of information sharing on terrorism and cross-border criminality between the EU bodies. This

and a concept of bringing terrorists to justice, e) the rapid sharing of policy information[3], and finally the paper suggests f) that the ability of terrorists "(…) to communicate and plan undetected should be impeded by measures such as the retention of telecommunications data" (Ibid. : 13) – all this " (…) while safeguarding data protection" (Ibid. : 13). As presented in chapter three, these arrangements are susceptible to being used in a manner that involves ethnic profiling, which does not necessarily mean that they always are. Paragraph 25 points out that a common understanding of the threat is crucial, so that a common political response to terrorist threats can be made (Ibid. : 12).

While establishing this 'common understanding of a threat', it is important to pay attention to the way data for the 'risk-assessment' is collected and analyzed. The differentiation of tolerable Islam and intolerable, fundamentalist Islam, for example, is part of the protection of the German constitution. A clear distinction like that could lead to more effective counter-terrorism and prevent certain groups of people from being under general suspicion. However, the presupposition, namely that a clear differentiation of threatening and tolerable Islam is even possible, suggests that there are no stages of transition, which in fact exist. Furthermore, not all the members of an organization which is classified as fundamental support the organization's opinion. These arguments suggest that this clear distinction has only been drawn for bureaucratic reasons. Werner Schiffauer, who specialized in research on Muslim communities, found out that the collected data by means of which the classification was made, was not based on broad studies. Moreover, analysts were not allowed to mingle with the observed people during the phase of data collection. The classification is therefore based on written sources, which might lead to a different outcome from a holistic research approach (Schiffauer 2006 : 2ff).

---

involved the implementation of biometric data and the access to that by all the Member States. He also confirmed the urgency to realize the Hague Program (Schily 2005 : 9f).

[3] All these suggestions are phrased in points 21ff (Ibid. : 11ff)

5.2 European Legal Standards Concerning Ethnic Profiling

Sensitive data, including information on ethnicity, may be gathered in numerous contexts, at aliens departments, or at places of employment and education. It can lawfully be gathered for purposes of ethnic monitoring, as long as it happens with the individual's consent. However, in the police sector, the conditions on the collection of sensitive data and limits of its use are not codified yet (Hayes 2005 : 32).

Paragraph 31 of the EU Counter-Terrorism Strategy summarizes that one of the key priorities on 'Pursue' are to "(e)nsure full implementation and evaluation of existing legislation as well as the ratification of relevant international Treaties and Conventions" (European Council Document 14469/04/05 REV 4: 14). This ensured that the EU would provide a common legal framework. However, none of the recently provided treaties and conventions included an explicit norm or law on the interdiction of ethnic profiling and existing official statements on data protection or the use of such profiling are only casually taken into account. Some of these statements and recommendations are specified in the following paragraphs.

The Council of Europe (COE) Convention of 1981 decided on the 'Protection of Individuals with regard to Automatic Processing of Personal Data' that collection of data, storage, use and access to it have to be restricted. Article 8 of the European Convention on Human Rights says that personal "(…) data revealing racial origin, political opinions or religious and other beliefs, as well as personal data concerning health or sexual life, may not be processed automatically unless domestic law provides appropriate safeguards." (1981 COE Convention: Chapter II, Art. 6). However,

> "(d)erogation from the provisions of Articles 5, 6 and 8 of this convention shall be allowed when such derogation (…) constitutes a necessary measure in a democratic society in the interests of: protecting State security, public safety, the monetary interests of the State or the suppression of criminal offences;" (Ibid. Art. 9)

This means that the article grants exemption for the police. A further COE recommendation in 1987 was another attempt to regulate the use of personal data by the police by introducing time limits, data security and notification of the data subjects. It restricted the exchange of information with other public bodies and recommended to prohibit the use of sensitive data, unless it was prescribed by law. However, COE recommendations are non-binding (Hayes 2005 : 33).

To ensure the implementation of the 1981 COE Convention, the European Commission proposed binding EU legislation in 1990. In 1995 the COE Convention was finally transposed into the Directive 1995/46/EC on the 'Protection of Individuals with regard to the Processing of Personal Data and the Free Movement of Such Data', which even broadened the exemptions, including all "(…) processing operations concerning public security, defense, State security (…) and the activities of the State in areas of criminal law" (EC Directive 1995/46/EC: Art. 3). The final draft, however, was never adopted.

In 2002 the EU updated and amended an earlier directive 1997/66/EC concerning the processing of personal data and the protection of privacy in the telecommunications sector. "The update removed the crucial obligation on service providers to erase communications traffic data immediately after it has been used for billing purposes" (Hayes 2005 : 35). The latest amendments on that directive were made in 2006. The 'Directive on the retention of data generated or processed in connection with the provision of publicly available electronic communications services or of public communications networks' reaffirmed the need for common measures on the retention of telecommunications data in the wake of the London bombings. Article 11 allows access to the retained data for investigation, detection and prosecution of criminal offenses and puts emphasis on the

> "(...) need to ensure at European level that data that are generated or processed, in the course of the supply of communications services, by providers of publicly available electronic communications services or of a public communications network are retained for a certain period, subject to the conditions provided for in this Directive." (EC Directive 2006/24/EC: Art. 11)

However, the case of ethnic profiling does not only concern the domain of data protection, but also pertains to legal norms on discrimination. The United Nations (UN), the Council of Europe – the Committee on the Elimination of Racial Discrimination (CERD) and the European Commission against Racism and Intolerance (ECRI) have stated that non-discrimination is a jus cogens-norm that does not allow curtailing – not even in the case of terrorism. This implies that ethnic profiling violates the prohibition against discrimination. Article five of the UN Convention on the elimination of all Forms of Racial Discrimination constitutes this claim with: "The right to equal treatment before the tribunals and all other organs administering justice;" (UN Race Convention: Art. 5 a) as well as several other political rights, most notably: "The right to freedom of movement and residence within the border of the State;" (Ibid. : Art. 5 d (i)) and "The right to freedom of thought, conscience and religion;" (Ibid. : Art. 5 d (vii)). The International Covenant on Civil and Political Rights (ICCPR), which is based on the Universal Declaration of Human Rights, says similarly in Article 9.1: "Everyone has the right to liberty and security of person. No one shall be subjected to arbitrary arrest or detention. No one shall be deprived of his liberty except on such grounds and in accordance with such procedure as are established by law" (ICCPR: Art. 9.1) And the Program of Action of the 2000 UN World Conference against Racism urges:

> "(…) States to design, implement and enforce effective measures to eliminate the phenomenon popularly known as "racial profiling" and comprising the practice of police and other law enforcement officers relying, to any degree, on race, colour, descent or national or ethnic origin as the basis for subjecting persons to investigatory activities or for determining whether an individual is engaged in criminal activity;" (UN 2001 : 33)

In 2003, the CERD demanded "(…) that States and international organizations ensure that measures taken in the struggle against terrorism do not discriminate in purpose or effect on grounds of race, colour, descent, or national or ethnic origin;" (CERD Document CERD/C/62/Misc.24: Paragraph 5). One year later, the 'CERD recommendation on the discrimination against non-citizens formally advised against ethnic profiling by recommending states to

> "(e)nsure that any measures taken in the fight against terrorism do not discriminate, in purpose or effect, on the grounds of race, colour, descent, or national or ethnic origin and that non-citizens are not subjected to racial or ethnic profiling or stereotyping;" (CERD Gen. Rec. No. 30: Art. 2.10).

Furthermore it says in 'CERD recommendation 31 on the prevention of racial discrimination in the administration and functioning of the criminal justice system' that

> "(s)tates parties should take the necessary steps to prevent questioning, arrests and searches which are in reality based solely on the physical appearance of a person, that person's colour or features or membership of a racial or ethnic group, or any profiling which exposes him or her to greater suspicion." (CERD Gen. Rec. No. 31: Art. 3.20)

Similarly, the ECRI's 2004 'General Policy Recommendation No. 8 on Combating Racism while Fighting Terrorism' urges states to implement legislation adopted in connection with counter-terrorism at national and local level in a manner that "(…) does not discriminate against persons or groups of persons, notably on grounds of actual or supposed "race", colour, language, religion, nationality, national or ethnic origin;" (ECRI Gen. Pol. Rec. No. 8: 5). It also demands

> "(…) to pay particular attention to guaranteeing in a non discriminatory way the freedoms of association, expression, religion and movement and to ensuring that no discrimination ensues from legislation and regulations – or their implementation – notably governing the following areas: checks carried out by law enforcement officials within the countries and by border control personnel (...) protection of personal data etc." (ECRI Gen. Pol. Rec. No. 8: 5)

The UN Code of Conduct for Law Enforcement Officials urges such officials to "(…) maintain and uphold the human rights of all persons" (UN Document A/RES/34/169: Art.2). The same is done by the European Code of Police Ethics of the Council of Europe, which asks the police to carry out their tasks guided by the principle of impartiality and non-discrimination. Police investigation shall be objective, fair and based on reasonable suspicion of an actual or possible offense. (European Code of Police Ethics: Para. 40ff).

However at the 2008 CERD Convention on the Elimination of all Forms of Racial Discrimination the committee noted

> "(…) with concern that despite the measures adopted at the federal and state levels to combat racial profiling (...) such practice continues to be widespread. In particular, the Committee is deeply

concerned about the increase in racial profiling against Arabs, Muslims and South Asians in the wake of the 9/11 attack, as well as about the development of the National Entry and Exit Registration System (NEERS) for nationals of 25 countries, all located in the Middle East, South Asia or North Africa." (CERD Document CERD/C/USA/CO/6: 14)

5.3 Weighing the Arguments: the Principle of Proportionality

It is a legitimate aim for the state – if not a core function – to take measures for its protection against internal or external threats to its existence, to the security of its citizens or its independence. Since terrorist activity might lead to mass murder – one of the most serious consequences of committed crimes, it is important for security measures to be far-reaching. Therefore preventive arrangements might affect innocent people. Given that the prevailing terrorism is religiously and politically motivated and governments claim that terrorist 'sleepers' are most likely to be Muslim, it seems to be a matter of course that the people disproportionately concerned by preventive counter-terrorism are Middle Eastern or South Asian men. Distinctions on the basis of race, national origin or religion do not violate the key principle of non-discrimination as such, which is anchored in any legal system. Taking the example of criminal profiling, classifications by characteristic traits for law enforcement purposes are inevitable or essential when used in descriptive profiling (s. chapter 2.2). If such criteria are supported by objective and reasonable grounds, their use is conducive.

However, the European Court of Human Rights (ECHR) stated that: "[T]he exigencies of dealing with terrorist crime cannot justify stretching the notion of 'reasonableness' to the point where the essence of the safeguard secured by Article 5 para. 1 (c) is impaired" (ECHR in COE 2002 : 24). Still, states enjoy a relatively wide margin[4] when it comes to national

[4] There is a tendency of a shift away from the wide margin, since the national security is a public interest and this considered to be matter of elected representatives rather than unelected judges. A second argument refers to the better ability that other branches (but law) have to evaluate the risk of differential treatment and national security. Thus, courts are usually not involved in political processes for reasons of neutrality. Furthermore, judicial decisions rely on special, precisely developed procedures to evaluate problems from a juridical

security. But as pointed out earlier, there is permissible and impermissible differential treatment of which the latter has serious effects on the disproportionately treated individuals. This matter is increasingly becoming the concern of stringent review, since courts acknowledge that liberty and security are closely interlinked. This coherency has been elaborated in detail in the last few chapters. The 'burden of proof', namely that differential treatment under certain circumstances is justifiable, is here shifted to the state (Moeckli[5] 2008 : 88). Certain grounds for differential treatment need to be assessed with particular scrutiny, such as race, religion and nationality. Since there is a prohibition of discrimination on the basis of race, this case is very difficult to justify. The European Court of Human Rights stated in Hoffman v Austria that "(...) (n)otwithstanding any possible arguments to the contrary, a distinction based essentially on a difference in religion alone is not acceptable" (ECHR Doc. 17 E.H.R.R. 293: para. 36). According to the UN Human Rights Committee, distinctions on the basis of nationality are in violation of Article 26 of the ICCPR and in Germany citizenship and nationality are tested under the equality clause of Article 3(1) of the Grundgesetz, which entails strict scrutiny (Moeckli 2008 : 81f).

To assess the states' margin, the proportionality test was introduced. It is a procedure to gradually find out, if the government's means to fulfill an objective infringe upon constitutional rights. The proportionality test is therefore a crucial part for judicial review and a general principle throughout the ECHR, it is also part of the discrimination test employed by the UN Human Rights Committee (Ibid. : 77). It encompasses several judicial situations or questions that are iterated.

The first question is, if the act under question was intentionally or indirectly discriminatory. Indirect discrimination is the seemingly equal treatment generating disproportionate effects. So the effects can be indicators. This suggests that discrimination can be established regardless of the states intention, which is equally prohibited in the EU. To find out if a certain act has generated indirect discrimination, analogous situations in which

view (Moeckli 2008 : 85ff).

[5] Daniel Moeckli (PhD) read law at the University of Berne in Switzerland, where he also qualified as a Barrister and Solicitor. He published several essays on the right to non-discrimination in the 'war on terror' from a juridical perspective. In some of his considerations he also uses the proportionality test.

people were treated differently (or different situations in which people were treated equally) need to be compared (Ibid. : 74ff). If this comparison leads to the insight that analogous situations were treated differently, the next step is to find out, if there was a reasonable justification, a legitimate aim, for the differential treatment. However, some authors have "(…) criticized the legitimate aim test as being a mere rhetorical assertion and redundant. Certainly in the case of anti-terrorism measures, states will usually be able to meet this requirement quite easily by referring to national security interests" (Ibid. : 77).

Even if the differential treatment was connected to a legitimate aim, there is still the need to balance individual rights and the interests of the community. To weigh this balance carefully, the criterion of proportionality is subdivided in three steps: 1. Suitability – the (disproportionate) means need to be suitable and effective to achieve the aim. 2. Necessity – there are no less restrictive (or disproportionate) measures available to achieve the aim. 3. Proportionality in the narrow sense – the disadvantage imposed on individuals must not be disproportionate to the importance of the aim, which means that the criterion on which the differential treatment is based is not over- or under-inclusive. This balancing element also takes into consideration "(…) the negative implications of the measure in question, including (…) the impacts it has on the affected groups. Thus, what are possible negative effects – or, in other words, the costs – of anti-terrorism measures that involve differential treatment of certain groups of people" (Ibid. : 79)? With this, a central problem of this thesis, namely the implications of ethnic profiling, is related to a juridical method designed to assess the (legal) consequences of its deployment.

The United Nations Office of the High Commissioner for Human Rights devised a principle, which can be drawn upon while balancing the states' duty to respond to national security threats and the individuals' fundamental rights:

> "The principle of non-discrimination must always be respected and special efforts made to safeguard the rights of vulnerable groups. Counter-terrorism measures targeting specific ethnic or religious groups are contrary to human rights and would carry the additional risk of an upsurge of discrimination and racism." (UNOHCHR 2003 : 5)

This means that using ethnic profiling in counter-terrorism should be effective, have few negative effects and achieve results that could not be produced without ethnic profiling. Furthermore, the amount of discrimination produced while implementing it should not outweigh the aim.

Testing Ethnic Profiling in Counter-Terrorism

To assess whether ethnic profiling is intentionally or indirectly discriminatory, one has to refer to the effects on the different groups need to be made. None of the documents on terrorist profiling or public debates on ethnic profiling state that European counter-terrorism measures are intentionally discriminatory. Proponents of profiling generally refrain from this kind of criticism and take trouble in centering the non-discriminatory practice of profiling and its effectiveness. However, the differential treatment of ethnic minority and majority groups is part of the logic of ethnic profiling. Taking into consideration that randomized searches or behavioral profiles could be an alternative, and therewith a shift away from differential treatment of different ethnicities is possible, ethnic profiling can be considered a discriminatory practice. It furthermore infringes on the individual's right to equal treatment before organs administering justice and the right to freedom of movement, just to name a few of the individual rights pointed out in chapter 5.2 on legal standards. So if this cannot be considered intentional discrimination, the differential treatment leads at least to indirect discrimination.

Hereupon, some proponents refer to statistical discrimination: a certain ethnic group is profiled because they bear a significant proportion of terrorist offenders. As terrorists are 'at war' with the attacked country they must belong to a certain ethnicity or religion, just like the attackers of 9/11 and the London and Madrid bombings. To not waste law-enforcement energy, ethnicity has to be taken into account. However, as pointed out in chapter 4.2 on over-inclusion, not only the overwhelming majority of the profiled group is innocently put under general suspicion (and is therefore discriminated against), but also the descriptive profile is in this case used indirectly for predictive profiling. Hence follow wrongful accusations and arrests with profound consequences for the profiled individuals. Furthermore, the significance of the factor ethnicity has to be evaluated. The data taken from a few terrorist incidents might not be enough to verify a significant correlation of race and terrorism. Therefore, the proponents' argument tends to rest on broad generalizations. Preconceptions of the connection between ethnicity and terrorism need to be tested and profound research in Muslim communities has to be done. Possible correlations with other factors need to be taken into account. The most striking argument for over-inclusion is the conflation of race and religion. Race is used as an indicator for jihadi terrorism. However, Muslim religion is not limited to certain ethnicities and only 7 percent of all Muslims belong to radical Islam. Furthermore, ethnic profiling in this case focuses on jihadi terrorism. However, as indicated in chapter 4.2 on under-inclusion, the majority of terrorist activities in Europe are Basque or Separatist.

The disproportionate and discriminating practice of ethnic profiling may be justified with a legitimate aim, while the amount of discrimination is proportional to the aim. The aim of ethnic profiling in counter-terrorism is obvious and legitimate: averting terrorist attacks for the security of a country and its people. It is not only a legitimate aim, but also a very important one. It is even the government's responsibility to fight terrorism.

However, it is imperative to discuss if ethnic profiling is a suitable, necessary and proportional means to counter terrorism. Concerning the suitability of ethnic profiling, proponents argue that the increased attention of law enforcement on the high-offending minority group leads to more detection of terrorists among that group; in short: ethnic profiling leads to an increased success rate, attacks are averted and possible future attacks prevented by the incapacitation of terrorists. Due to the deterring effect of profiling (target hardening), raids and further police actions, fewer members of the high-offending minority group engage in terrorist activities.

However, in chapter 4.1 on the deterring effects of ethnic profiling, it has been pointed out that this holds true for the immediate aftermath of the implementation of the measure (primary effects of ethnic profiling). The central question is, if this benefit outweighs the following disadvantages: the profile can be circumvented by substitution. Apart from the possibility of switching to a different terrorist instrument or strategy, the actors, either consciously or because of social development, may recruit attackers who do not fit the profile, for example women. Examples of this process were given in chapter 4.2 on substitution. According to the high-offending group's elasticity, the overall amount of terrorism might fall (in case of normal elasticity) or rise (in case of low elasticity). If one assumes that the offending rate of a group is higher, why should they be more or as elastic to policing than members of the low-offending group? In this case profiling and further repressive counter-terrorism measures will increase the overall amount of terrorism. Furthermore, strict ethnic profiling shifts law enforcement officers' and intelligence's attention away from behavioral aspects of terrorism, which could be more effective. So ethnic profiling would then not just be an unsuitable means, but also counterproductive. It is not effective, since it has a relatively huge margin of error (over-inclusion), it rarely produces concrete results (s. German dragnet investigation): the general crime rate might rise, because law enforcement resources are shifted away from general crime to terrorism and it requires considerable financial resources, if connected to data mining or similar procedures.

Ethnic profiling might, however, produce collateral benefits, such as the disclosure of immigration offenses. But the fact that individuals are singled out on the basis of their ethnicity is discrimination and leads to frustration. These experiences on the singular level are translated into group effects. Generalizations and biased media coverage promote a negative stereotype of the group and put it under general suspicion, which is likely to result in societal Islamophobia. This stigma, again, leads to the alienation of the community, as well as mistrust and tensions between the group and the representatives of the state.

Furthermore, ethnic profiling is likely to result in a self-confirming prophecy. The disproportional law enforcement contact of the profiled minority group creates what was introduced as the ratchet effect in chapter 4.3 and its social after-effects. Strain and defiance are possible reactions to disproportional law enforcement contacts and alienation. Strain and defiance are likely to aggravate the general situation as they might result in a higher crime rate and attacks (expression of defiance). The prospects of the co-operation of the targeted group with police, as well as its integration recede.

The preceding arguments suggest that ethnic profiling cannot be considered as a suitable means to counter terrorism. It is disproportionate since it affects a lot of innocent people and entails considerable social and monetary costs. The aim itself does not legitimize the discriminatory practice. At this point, the proportionality test would come to an end, since the criterion 'suitability' is not met. And if one criterion is not met, there is no need for further discussion of the other criteria. However, a couple of considerations concerning the other points should still be mentioned. Some authors argue that there is also no necessity to deploy ethnic profiling in counter-terrorism, since the focus on behavioral and psycho-social aspects of religious or otherwise motivated terrorism could be more efficient and less discriminatory. However, these measures require more and profounder research into terrorism.

Another possibility of less discriminatory counter-terrorism efforts with fewer negative secondary effects and repercussions on security policy are randomized searches on airports, on the street etc. This will be further discussed as an option in the conclusion and the exposition of future prospects.

As already pointed out in the discussion on the criterion ‘suitability’, the proportionality in the narrow sense is not met, either, since ethnic profiling and its possible repercussions can be considered counterproductive. However, this does not mean that ethnicity cannot be part of profiles in general. If a profile is exclusively descriptive, it is the law enforcement officer’s duty to take details on ethnicity into consideration. Anything else would be counterproductive in finding and suing terrorists.

6. DRAWING CONCLUSIONS

Towards Non-Discriminatory Police Actions in Counter-Terrorism

The preceding argumentation yields considerations for future prospects in various domains. Conclusions can be drawn for the general utilization of profiling in the counter-terrorism context, for relevant legal frameworks, for counter-terrorism policies and for the conduct of law enforcement officers in that context.

Future Prospects for Security Checks and the Practice of Profiling

Target hardening is undoubtedly an important aspect of countering terrorism. It can be realized by means of security controls, and there are several options to prevent these from becoming discriminatory. The first option is to introduce universal controls. This might indeed be effective, but it is structurally almost impossible to implement on the street. It works, however, in closed settings, such as airports. Security controls are already universally implemented on all European airports.

However, as pointed out in chapter two, profiling is a measure to facilitate law enforcement effort by selecting those individuals for controls who are most likely to be involved in terrorism. But universal controls are not based on profiling at all. One measure to minimize law enforcement efforts is randomized searches. If individuals are selected randomly, instead of on an ethnic basis, discrimination can structurally not occur. Another advantage of randomized searches is that it excludes the possibility of individuals circumventing a profile. Random searches could affect everyone equally, so they are also not based on a profile.

A third option is to put more weight on intelligence-led profiling. These profiles may include behavioral and psychological characteristics. Behavioral aspects could be: a) certain places being monitored by strangers, b) someone trying to gain information on critical infrastructures, c) the penetration of physical security barriers to check the time it takes for a security response, or d) the purchasing of supplies (like explosives, weapons, ammunition, chemicals) (Secure Community Network 2005 : 1)[1]. Behavioral

[1] Whereas investing into intelligence has the advantage of being mostly 'invisible', it is important to stress that the increased use of technology to

characteristics could also encompass more specific situational aspects as described in chapter 2.1 on the genesis of criminal profiling[2]. A behavioral profile is still possible to circumvent, however. Any profile can be substituted. Behavioral profiling is simply a possibility that does not intrude on a person's right to non-discrimination.

The classification of 'dangerous' groups may also be part of psychological or behavioral profiling, however, the research into and the gathering of information on these groups should be deepened, and monitored at the same time, as suggested by Werner Schiffauer. He pointed out that the research that led to the classification of dangerous groups by the German protection of the constitution was not adequate and linked to distorting guidelines (Schiffauer 2006 : 244ff). To focus on behavioral aspects, it is important to put more weight on researching the practice of terrorist profiling on the one hand and the profiled groups on the other. This is not to say that there has not been a lot of research done and directed in all the European countries. However, there is very little knowledge about elasticity and substitution effects in counter-terrorism up to now. The same holds true for the evaluation of defensive counter-terrorism measures in general (Harcourt 2006 : 28). Even though most of the theories exposed in this thesis were substantiated with examples of counter-terrorism practice, some approaches contain speculative elements. It is therefore important to support empirical research on the implications of ethnic profiling and other counter-terrorism efforts that may be revealed as discriminatory.

Strengthening Legal Standards

One could draw upon a number of laws and directives in the debate on ethnic profiling. However, there is no existing law that forbids ethnic profiling as such. Passing a law on the prohibition of ethnic profiling would of course be the most drastic, as well as the most effective, solution. It was highlighted by different parties that ethnic profiling is discriminatory.

---

monitor some behavioral aspects could also increase the overall amount of surveillance and visible security measures.

[2] (1) the buying of tickets with large amounts of cash; (2) traveling under a different name; (3) traveling to suspicious so-called 'drug-source cities'; (4) staying at a destination only for a few hours; (5) appearing nervous; (6) not checking in any luggage (Harris 2002 : 20)

The discriminatory practice of law enforcement could furthermore affect the elasticity of the profiled group. Harcourt, for example, refers to Tom Tyler's theory on democratic governance and the importance of procedural justice (s. chapter 4.1 on defiance). Illegitimate measures might affect peoples' trust in, and consequently their obedience to, the law (Harcourt 2006 : 28). Even if these statements only rest on assumptions, there are a number of organizations and authors that promote the proactive human rights approach combined with a clear legal framework:

> "Insisting that the fight against terrorism be based on formal rules that are equally applicable to everyone – on rules that meet Kant's requirement of universality – would serve as an important safeguard against the common tendency to associate terrorism with a certain category of persons and to pit 'us' against 'them'."(Moeckli 2008 : 235)

Oliver De Schutter, professor of law at Belgium's University of Louvain and a specialist in human rights legislation, argues for

> "(…) the passage of laws that sufficiently hem in or even forbid the use of profiling, and new rules that impose transparency and systematic independent evaluation of police techniques to ensure they do not cross the line into illegal or disproportionate use of profiling as the basis for action." (De Schutter in Tigner 2007 : 1)

The Leadership Conference on Civil Rights Education demand in their paper a legally enforceable ban of ethnic profiling including a clear definition of ethnic profiling (Leadership Conference on Civil Rights Education Fund 2003 : 33). This, again, supports Moeckli's demand that

> "(…) international and regional human rights bodies as well as those bodies that are charged with monitoring and coordinating the implementation of international obligations to counter terrorism, should adopt a proactive approach and send a clear signal to states that law enforcement practices adopted in the anti-terrorism context must comply with human rights standards, including the principle of non-discrimination." (Moeckli 2006 : 23)

The creation of a clear legal framework is also supported by the CERD Convention 2008:

> "Bearing in mind its general recommendation No. 31 (2005) on the prevention of racial discrimination in the administration and functioning of the criminal justice system, the Committee recommends that the State party strengthen its efforts to combat racial profiling at the federal and state levels, inter alia by moving expeditiously towards the adoption of the End Racial Profiling Act, or similar federal legislation. The Committee also draws the attention of the State party to its general recommendation no. 30 (2004) on discrimination against non-citizens, according to which measures taken in the fight against terrorism must not discriminate, in purpose or effect, on the grounds of race, colour, descent, or national or ethnic origin, and urges the State party, in accordance with article 2, paragraph 1 (c), of the Convention, to put an end to the National Entry and Exit Registration System (NEERS) and to eliminate other forms of racial profiling against Arabs, Muslims and South Asians" (CERD Convention 2008 : 14)

All these statements make clear that legal standards (regulations) against ethnic profiling need to be established, in the first instance by the European Council or by binding legislation on a national level. Any laws that are of significant concern for the freedom of movement and the freedom of expression should be debated in less closed institutions, as some authors demand, since anti-terror laws on the access and gathering of passenger data, biometrics collection or profiling, are routinely used for other lawful purposes too, and affect everyone (Privacy International 2005 : 8f). The mutual benefits of ethnic profiling in counter-terrorism and immigration policy underscores this assumption.

Monitoring the Police

The monitoring of law enforcement officials is a crucial part of the research into the implementation of ethnic profiling. Collecting information on the impact of their techniques and the techniques themselves, could help to find out if the police is indeed bigoted in profiling. In the UK for example, Stop and Searches on Terrorism Act 2000 are counted with reference to the searched individual's ethnicity. Statistics on the outcomes of those stops could support an internal police analysis of the productivity of stops, enhancing supervision and efficient resource allocation (Goldston

2006 : 14). As De Shutter puts it: "Police and law enforcement authorities have a tendency to protect themselves from criticism. But we have to force them to become more transparent" (De Schutter in Tigner 2007 : 2). Other authors demand more than transparency: the possibility for victims to complain about disproportionate law enforcement should be taken seriously (Leadership Conference on Civil Rights Education Fund 2003 : 33). Furthermore, law enforcement officers should be held accountable for violations of human rights (Moeckli 2006 : 24). Disciplinary measures have been successfully implemented in some cases, for example, when Mr. Robert Underhill had successfully sued New South Wales Police for wrongful arrest and false imprisonment (New South Wales Council for Civil Liberties inc. 2006 : 1) or Mr. Adam Houda, a Muslim lawyer, who sued the Australian Police for wrongful arrest, malicious prosecution and false imprisonment (Wallace : 2005 : 1f).

In accordance with a new law, training standards for police authorities should help law enforcement officers to develop a 'best practice'-attitude, making clear that ethnic profiling does not comply with human rights standards. Funding for technology that can verify the accuracy of data collected by law enforcement officers as well as for the creation of an early warning system and feedback systems that identify officers in danger of racial profiling, should be secured (Leadership Conference on Civil Rights Education Fund 2003 : 34).

Political Matters

Ethnic profiling is one attempt to regulate terrorism. According to John Braithwaite's (2005) model of the Integration of Restorative, Deterrent and Incapacitative Justice, however, the maximum harm reduction in the war against terror is achieved with dialogue, reconciliation and creative problem solving. He argues that restorative justice is the most socially responsible way of countering terrorism. As opposed to deterrence and incapacitation, which cause more harm than good, and therefore also lead to defiant reactions. Any kind of profiling can be affiliated to 'deterrence'. To support this theory, Braithwaite draws upon the fact that

> "(m)ost bouts of terrorism in the twentieth century, after all, had ended with the integration of some terrorist leaders into democratic power structures – whether it was Northern Ireland terrorism,

> Israeli terrorism, South African terrorism, East Timorese terrorism, the terrorism of the Italian Red Brigades or of the Bader-Meinhof gang in Germany (…). Mustapha Al Sayyid (2003) has attempted to show that the evidence is that Islamist organisations are more successful when they reject violence in favor of electoral politics. Al Quaeda's appeal will collapse only when Muslims who believe in the ideal of an Islamic state turn on al Quaeda for using un-Islamic means for achieving the end they share (…). Of course the more injustice and humiliation the West hurls at Islamists, the less likely such a marginalisation of al Queada will become." (Braithwaite 2005 : 104)

According to this logic, ethnic profiling is conducive to the tightening of the overall situation. As already brought up in chapter four, a stable integration of minorities into wider societies would already help to prevent frustration in members of the minority group. As opposed to discriminatory and alienating ethnic profiling, the collaboration of police and minority communities supports mutual trust and strengthens the minority group's obedience to the law. "The challenges inherent in building partnerships are significant; there is little history of Muslim community-police cooperation in many European countries, and outright hostility among some. These will have to be addressed head-on" (Goldston 2006 : 14).

The political impact that ethnic profiling has on Muslim communities is very strong. It is therefore even more worrisome that ethnic profiling seems to be, in turn, a "(…) consequence of conscious decisions taken within a general climate that favors the targeting of particular marginal groups" (Moeckli 2006 : 23). Some law enforcement agencies do not only tolerate the use of ethnic profiling, but also encourage it. As long as these practices enjoy public support, ethnic profiling will be a politically convenient strategy to demonstrate the law enforcement effort on counter-terrorism (Ibid. : 23). This however, can be redressed by a public education campaign[3] that explains the false conclusions of ethnic profiling and highlights its counterproductive and discriminatory aspects. In the same way, the media

---

[3] This kind of campaign was already suggested at the Leadership Conference on Civil Rights Education in 2003 (Leadership Conference on Civil Rights Education Fund 2003 : 35).

coverage on this topic should increasingly be adjusted and examples of 'best practice' publicly evaluated.

As it was discussed in this thesis, the utilization of ethnic profiling in counter-terrorism is a complex problem. Therefore, a combination of the options for action mentioned above should be considered to ensure that European counter-terrorism measures are non-discriminatory.

REFERENCES

ADEL, Z. (2002): *Muslime wehren sich gegen unrechtmässige Moschee-durchsuchungen.*
Available at: http://www.islam.de/2522.php (15.07.2008)

AGNEW, R. (1999): *A General Strain Theory of Community Differences in Crime Rates.* In: *Journal of Research in Crime and Delinquency 36 (2):* 123-155.

ARTICLE 29 DATA PROTECTION WORKING PARTY (2005): *Document 1022/05/EN WP 110 „Opinion 2/2005 on the Proposal for a Regulation of the European Parliament and of the Council concerning the Visa Information System (VIS) and the exchange of data between Member States on short stay-visas. 23 June 2005".*
Available at: http://ec.europa.eu/justice_home/fsj/privacy/docs/wp-docs/2005/wp110_en.pdf (02.08.2008)

ASSOCIATION OF PAROLING AUTHORITIES INTERNATIONAL (APAI) AND THE NATIONAL INSTITUTE OF CORRECTIONS (2003): *Handbook for New Parole Board Members.*
Available at: http://www.apaintl.org/content/en/pdf/CEPPParoleHandbook.pdf (11.07.2008)

THE ASSOCIATED PRESS (2007): *EU, U.S. agree on sharing air passenger data.*
Available at: http://www.usatoday.com/travel/flights/2007-06-29-passenger-data_N.htm (20.07.2008)

BBC NEWS (2001a): *Passenger profiling: A security option?*
Available at: http://news.bbc.co.uk/2/hi/uk_news/1726966.stm (20.07.2008)

BBC NEWS (2001b): *Hijack ‚suspects' alive and well.*
Available at: http://news.bbc.co.uk/2/hi/middle_east/1559151.stm (22.08.2008)

BBC NEWS (2001c): *Profile: Timothy McVeigh.*
Available at: http://news.bbc.co.uk/2/hi/americas/1321244.stm (05.09.2008)

BBC NEWS (2002): *German police raid mosque.*
Available at: http://news.bbc.co.uk/2/hi/europe/2250590.stm (22.07.2008)

BBC NEWS (2005a): *Madrid bombing suspects.*
Available at: http://news.bbc.co.uk/2/hi/europe/3560603.stm (22.08.2008)

BBC NEWS (2005b): *21 July London bombings suspects.*
Available at: http://news.bbc.co.uk/2/hi/uk_news/4721645.stm (22.08.2008)

BBC NEWS (2007): *Italy police raid ‚terror school'.*
Available at: http://news.bbc.co.uk/2/hi/europe/6909961.stm (20.07.2008)

BBC NEWS (2008a): *EU tightens anti-terrorism laws.*
Available at: http://news.bbc.co.uk/2/hi/europe/7355446.stm (17.08.2008)

BBC NEWS (2008b): *Student was ‚studying terrorism'.*
Available at: http://news.bbc.co.uk/2/hi/uk_news/england/nottinghamshire/7415685.stm (27.08.2008)

BBC NEWS (2008c): *Deadly Jerusalem bulldozer attack.*
Available at: http://news.bbc.co.uk/2/hi/middle_east/7485022.stm (29.08.2008)

BECKER, H.S. (1963): *Outsiders: Studies in the Sociology of Deviance.* New York.

BECTON, C. L. (1987): *The Drug Courier Profile: ‚All Seems Infected That th' Infected Spy, as All Looks Yellow to the Jaundic'd Eye'.* In: *North Carolina Law Review 65:* 417-81.

BIRT, Y. (2008): *Just how big a threat is ‚Islamic' terrorism?*
Available at: http://www.yahyabirt.com/?p=148 (11.09.2008)

BITTLE, S./JOHNSON, J. (2002): *Public Opinion: Racial Profiling and Islam at Home.*
Available at: http://www.publicagenda.com/specials/terrorism/terror_pubopinion9.htm (18.02.2008)

BNET (2007): *Security Roundup- Air Safety Week.*
Available at: http://findarticles.com/p/articles/mi_m0UBT/is_30_21/ai_n27333947 (19.07.2008)

BOSWELL, T./DIXON, W.J. (1990): *Dependency and Rebellion: a Crossnational Analysis.* In: *American Sociological Review 55 (4):* 540-559.

BRAITHWAITE, J. (2005): *Pre-empting Terrorism.* In: *Current Issues in Criminal Justice 17 (1):* 96-114.

BREHM, S.S./BREHM, J.W. (1981): *Psychological Reactance: A Theory of Freedom and Control.* New York.

BRIGHT, A. (2008): *Pilot wrongfully accused of 9/11 ties can seek damages from Britain.*
Available at: http://www.csmonitor.com/2008/0215/p99s01-duts.html (09.09.2008)

BROWN, G. (2007): *UK National Security Statement. 14 November 2007.* Available at: http://www.number10.gov.uk/Page13757 (13.08.2008)

CARLSON, D.K. (2004): *Racial Profiling Seen as Pervasive, Unjust.* Available at: http://www.gallup.com/poll/12406/Racial-Profiling-Seen-Pervasive-Unjust.aspx (11.09.2008)

CAULEY, J./IM, E. (1988): *Intervention Policy Analysis of Skyjackings and Other Terrorist Incidents.* In: *American Economic Review 78:* 27-31.

CITY OF LONDON POLICE (2007): *Stop and Search Figures – 1st of January to 31st December 2007.*
Available at: http://www.cityoflondon.police.uk/CityPolice/Utility/stopandsearch.htm (20.07.2008)

CHORLEY, M./LINDEN, M. (2006): *Top Muslim policeman attacks ‚terror profiling'.*
Available at: http://www.independent.co.uk/news/uk/crime/top-muslim-policeman-attacks-terror-profiling-412009.html (06.09.2008)

CNN.COM (2003): *‚Mini-arsenal' find at UK mosque.*
Available at: http://edition.cnn.com/2003/WORLD/europe/01/20/mosque.raid/ (20.07.2008)

COMMITTEE ON THE ELIMINATION OF RACIAL DISCRIMINATION (2003): *Document CERD/C/62/Misc.24 „Statement on racial discrimination and measures to combat terrorism.17 March 2003".*
Available at: http://www.unhchr.ch/tbs/doc.nsf/(Symbol)/CERD.C.62.Misc.24.En?Opendocument (06.08.2008)

COMMITTEE ON THE ELIMINATION OF RACIAL DISCRIMINATION (2004): *General Recommendation No.30 „Discrimination Against Non Citizens. 01 October 2004".*
Available at: http://www.unhchr.ch/tbs/doc.nsf/0/e3980a673769e229c1256f8d0057cd3d?Opendocument (06.08.2008)

COMMITTEE ON THE ELIMINATION OF RACIAL DISCRIMINATION (2005): *General Recommendation No. 31 „On the prevention of racial discrimination in the administration and functioning of the criminal justice system. 9 September 2005."*
Available at: http://www2.ohchr.org/english/bodies/cerd/docs/GC31Rev_En.pdf (06.08.2008)

COMMITTEE ON THE ELIMINATION OF RACIAL DISCRIMINATION (2008): *Document CERD/C/USA/CO/6 „International Convention on the Elimination of all Forms of Racial Discrimination. 7 March 2008".*
Available at: http://www1.umn.edu/humanrts/CERDConcludingComments2008.pdf (06.08.2008)

O'CONNOR, S. (2002): *Biometrics and Identification after 9/11.* In: *Bender's Immigration Bulletin 7:* 150- 173.

O'CONNOR, T. (2006): *Theories and Ideologies of Terrorism.*
Available at: http://www.apsu.edu/oconnort/3400/3400lect02.htm (18.08.2008)

COUNCIL OF EUROPE (1981): *Convention for the Protection of Individuals with regard of Automatic Processing of Personal Data. 28 January 1981.*
Available at: http://conventions.coe.int/Treaty/en/Treaties/Html/108.htm (04.08.2008)

COUNCIL OF EUROPE (2001): *Recommendation Rec (2001)10 „The European Code of Police Ethics. 19 September 2001".*
Available at: http://www.legislationline.org/legislation.php?lid=4886&tid=155 (07.08.2008)

COUNCIL OF EUROPE (2002): *Guidelines on human rights and the fight against terrorism adopted by the Committee of Ministers on 11 July 2002 at the 804th meeting of the Minister's Deputies.*
Available at: http://www1.umn.edu/humanrts/instree/HR%20and%20the%20fight%20against%20terrorism.pdf (11.08.2008)

COUNCIL OF THE EUROPEAN UNION (1995): *Document 95/46/EC „Directive on the protection of individuals with regard to the processing of personal data and on the free movement of such data. 24 October 1995".* Available at: http://eur-lex.europa.eu/smartapi/cgi/sga_doc?smartapi!celexapi!prod!CELEXnumdoc&lg=EN&numdoc=31995L0046&model=guichett (04.08.2008)

COUNCIL OF THE EUROPEAN UNION (1997): *Document 97/66/EC „Directive concerning the processing of personal data and the protection of privacy in the telecommunications sector. 15 December 1997".* Available at: http://eur-lex.europa.eu/LexUriServ/LexUriServ.do?uri=CELEX:31997L0066:EN:HTML (04.08.2008)

COUNCIL OF THE EUROPEAN UNION (2002): *Document 11858/3/02 REV 3 „Draft Council Recommendation on the development of terrorist profiles. 18 November 2002".* Available at: http://register.consilium.eu.int/pdf/en/02/st11/11858-r3en2.pdf (23.01.2008)

COUNCIL OF THE EUROPEAN UNION (2005): *Document 14469/4/05 REV 4 „The European Union Counter-Terrorism Strategy. 30 November 2005".* Available at: http://register.consilium.eu.int/pdf/en/05/st14/st14469-re04.en05.pdf (03.08.2008)

COUNCIL OF THE EUROPEAN UNION (2006): *Document 2006/24/EC „Directive on the retention of data generated or processed in connection with the provision of publicly available electronic communications services or of public communications networks and amending Directive 2002/58/EC. 13 April 2006".* Available at: http://eur-lex.europa.eu/LexUriServ/LexUriServ.do?uri=CELEX:32006L0024:EN:HTML (04.08.2008)

DEUTSCHE WELLE (DW)-WORLD.DE (2008): *Swedish Government Clears Hurdles to Pass Surveillance Bill.* Available at: http://www.dw-world.de/dw/article/0,2144,3421627,00.html (31.07.2008)

DODD, V. (2005): *Asian men targeted in stop and search. Huge rise in number questioned under anti-terror laws.*
Available at: http://www.guardian.co.uk/uk/2005/aug/17/race.july7/print (15.07.2008)

DODD, V./TRAVIS, A. (2005): *Muslims face increased stop and search.* Available at: http://www.guardian.co.uk/politics/2005/mar/02/terrorism.immigrationpolicy1/print

DPA (2005): *15 Millionen Muslime leben in der EU.*
Available at: http://www.tagesspiegel.de/politik/;art771,2077282 (22.08.2008)

ELLMANN, S. J. (2003): *Racial Profiling and Terrorism.* In: *New York Law School Law Review 46:* 675-730.

ENDERS, W./SANDLER, T. (1993): *The Effectiveness of Antiterrorism Policies: A Vector-Autoregression-Intervention Analysis.* In: *American Political Science Review 87 (4):* 829-844.

ENDERS, W./SANDLER, T. (2004): *What do We Know About the Substitution Effect In Transnational Terrorism?* In: SILKE, A./G. ILARDI (2004): *Researching Terrorism: Trends, Achievements, Failures.*
2002 Working Paper Available at: http://www-rcf.usc.edu/~tsandler/substitution2ms.pdf

ENGENE, J.O. (1998): *Patterns of Terrorism in Western Europe, 1950-95.* Bergen: Department of Comparative Politics, University of Bergen, doctoral dissertation.

EURACTIV (2007): *EU plans anti-terror screening for air passengers.* Available at: http://www.euractiv.com/en/transport/eu-plans-anti-terror-screening-air-passengers/article-168103 (19.07.2008)

EUROPA.EU (2006): *Aufnahme von biometrischen Daten in Pässe und Reisedokumente. 28 June 2006.*
Available at: http://europa.eu/scadplus/leg/de/lvb/l14154.htm (20.07.2008)

EUROPEAN COMMISSION (2005): *The Hague Program – Ten priorities for the next five years. 10 May 2005.*
Available at: http://ec.europa.eu/justice_home/news/information_dossiers/the_hague_priorities/index_en.htm (02.08.2008)

EUROPEAN COMMISSION (2007): *Document 0/243/2007 „Proposal for a Council Framework Decision on the use of Passenger Name Record (PNR) for law enforcement purposes. 22 October 2007".*
Available at: http://www.statewatch.org/news/2007/oct/eu-com-pnr-proposal.pdf (20.07.2008)

EUROPEAN COMMISSION AGAINST REACISM AND INTOLERANCE (2004): *ECRI General Policy Recommendation No. 8 „On Combating Racism while Fighting Terrorism. 14 March 2004".*
Available at: http://www.coe.int/t/e/human_rights/ecri/1-ecri/3-general_themes/1-policy_recommendations/recommendation_n8/recommendation_N%B0_8_eng.pdf (07.08.2008)

EUROPEAN COURT OF HUMAN RIGHTS (1993): *Document 17 E.H.R.R. 293 „Hoffmann v Austria".*
Available at: http://www.religlaw.org/template.php?id=143 (12.08.2008)

EUROPEAN UNION AGENCY FOR FUNDAMENTAL RIGHTS (2007): *Ethnic Profiling Project - Technical tender specifications / Terms of reference. Annex A.1 FRA2-2007-3200-T02.*
Available at: http://fra.europa.eu/fra/material/pub/calls/FRA2-2007-3200-T02/AnnexA1_TenderSpec_en.pdf (23.01.2008)

EUROPEAN UNION NETWORK OF INDEPENDENT EXPERTS IN FUNDAMENTAL RIGHTS (2003): *The Balance Between Freedom and Security in the Response by the European Union and its Member States to the Terrorist Threats. 31 March 2003.*
Available at: http://ec.europa.eu/justice_home/cfr_cdf/doc/obs_thematique_en.pdf (22.08.2008)

EUROPOL (2008): *TE-SAT 2008. EU Terrorism Situation and Trend Report. The Hague.*
Available at: http://www.europol.europa.eu/publications/EU_Terrorism_Situation_and_Trend_Report_TE-SAT/TESAT2008.pdf (15.09.2008)

FAY, J. (2007): *MEPs slate EU's terror assault on our data rights.*
Available at: http://www.theregister.co.uk/2007/12/13/meps_on_rights/ (20.07.2008)

FELSON, M. (1986): *Linking Criminal Choices, Routine Activities, Informal Control, and Criminal Outcomes.* In: D.B. CORNISH/R.V. CLARKE (1986): *The reasoning criminal: Rational choice perspectives on offending.* New York.

FORUM AGAINST ISLAMOPHOBIA AND RACISM (2004): *Counter-Terrorism Powers: Reconciling Security and Liberty in an Open Society: Discussion Paper – a Muslim Response.* Al Khoei Foundation and the Muslim College.

GILLAN, A./NORTON-TAYLOR, R./DODD, V. (2006): *Raided, arrested, released: the price of wrong intelligence.*
Available at: http://www.guardian.co.uk/uk/2006/jun/12/terrorism.politics (20.08.2008)

GOLDSTON, J. (2006): *Ethnic Profiling and Counter-Terrorism. Trends Dangers and Alternatives.*
Available at: http://www.soros.org/initiatives/osji/articles_publications/articles/counterterrorism_20060606 (22.07.2008)

GREEN, N. (2003): *Britain: Anti-terrorism sweep creates climate of fear.*
Available at: http://www.wsws.org/articles/2003/jul2003/terr-j23.shtml (20.08.2008)

GRÖTKER, R. (2002): *Eine kriminogenfreie Gesellschaft durch Data Mining?*
Available at: http://www.heise.de/tp/r4/artikel/11/11516/1.html (30.07.2008)

HARCOURT, B. E. (2006): *Muslim Profiles Post 9/11: Is Racial Profiling an Effective Counterterrorist Measure and does it violate the Right to be free from Discrimination?*
Available at: http://papers.ssrn.com/sol3/papers.cfm?abstract_id=893905 (18.08.2008)

HARCOURT, B. E. (2007): *Against Prediction. Profiling, Policing and Punishing in an Actuarial Age.* Chicago.

HARRIS, D. (2002): *Profiles in Injustice: Why racial profiling Cannot work.* New York.

HART, H. (1923): *Predicting Parole Success.* In: *Journal of the American Institute of Criminal Law and Criminology 41 (3):* 405-413.

HAYES, B. (2005): *A Failure to Regulate: Data Protection and Ethnic Profiling in the Police Sector in Europe.* In: OSI JUSTICE INTIATIVES, Ed. (2005): *Ethnic Profiling by Police in Europe.* New York: 32-43.

HEILIG, D. (2008): *Frontex macht die Grenzen dicht.*
Available at: http://www.neues-deutschland.de/artikel/131446.frontex-macht-die-grenzen-dicht.html (17.08.2008)

HOME OFFICE STATISTICAL BULLETIN (2008): *Crime in England and Wales 2007/08. Findings from the British Crime Survey and police recorded crime.*
Available at: http://www.homeoffice.gov.uk/rds/pdfs08/hosb0708.pdf (07.09.2008)

IGMG – DAS ISLAMISCHE PORTAL (2004): *Sture Polizeikontrollen in Niedersachsen gehen weiter.*
Available at: http://www.igmg.de/nachrichten/newsdetails/article/20/sture-polizeikontrollen-in-niedersachsen-gehen-weiter.html (22.07.2008)

IGMG – DAS ISLAMISCHE PORTAL (2005): *Willkürliche Polizeikontrollen in Niedersachsen halten an.*
Available at: http://www.igmg.de/nachrichten/newsdetails/article/20/willkuerliche-polizeikontrollen-in-niedersachsen-halten-an.html (22.07.2008)

INTERNATIONAL HELSINKI FEDERATION FOR HUMAN RIGHTS (2007): *Intolerance and Discrimination Against Muslims in the EU: Developments since September 11.*
Available at: http://www.ihf-hr.org/documents/doc_summary.php?sec_id=3&d_id=4029 (22.07.2008)

ISLAM.DE (2004): *Polizeigewalt gegen Fremde.* (15.07.2008)
Available at: http://www.islam.de/2529.php

JUNGE, B. (2008): *Lückenlose Kontrolle.*
Available at: http://www.tagesspiegel.de/politik/international/Terrorabwehr;art123,2484301 (20.07.2008)

KENNEDY, R. (1997): *Race, Crime and the Law.* New York.

KIRBY, T. (2005): *Muslim groups condemn stop-and-search policy.*
Available at: http://www.independent.co.uk/news/uk/crime/muslim-groups-condemn-stopandsearch-policy-501171.html

KITCHEN, S./MICHAELSON, J./WOOD, N. (2005): *Citizenship Survey: race and faith topic report. Department for Communities and Local Government 2006 :* 21-31.

KNIGHT, S. (2005): *Row over New Rules for Deporting Hate Preachers.* Available at: http://www.timesonline.co.uk/tol/news/uk/article558506.ece (05.09.2008)

KREMPL, S. (2008): *Citizen's rights activists intend to prevent EU plans to record passengers' flight details.*
Available at: http://www.heise.de/english/Citizen-s-rights-activists-intend-to-prevent-EU-plans-to-record-passengers-flight-details--/newsticker/news/101749 (20.07.2008)

LEADERSHIP CONFERENCE ON CIVIL RIGHTS EDUCATION FUND (2003): *Wrong then, wrong now. Racial Profiling Before and After September 11, 2001.*
Available at: http://www.civilrights.org/publications/reports/racial_profiling/racial_profiling_report.pdf (06.09.2008)

LEFKOVITS, E. (2008): *16 hurt in bulldozer attack in J'lem.*
Available at: http://www.jpost.com/servlet/Satellite?cid=1215331056523&pagename=JPost%2FJPArticle%2FShowFull (29.08.2008)

LEGGATT, J./S. ADDISON (2007): *Britain has longest terrorism detention.* Available at: http://uk.reuters.com/article/domesticNews/idUKL1257914520071112?pageNumber=2&virtualBrandChannel=0 (29.07.2008)

LEIKEN, R. (2004): *Bearers of Global Jihad? Immigration and National Security after 9/11.* The Nixon Center. Washington D.C.

LIA, B./SKJØLBERG, K. (2004): *Warum es zu Terrorismus kommt – Ein Überblick über Theorien und Hypothesen zu den Ursachen des Terrorismus.* In: *Journal für Konflikt- und Gewaltforschung 6 (1/2004):* 121-163.

LÖHE, F. (2008): *Nur jeder 14. Moslem ist radikal.*
Available at: http://www.focus.de/politik/ausland/tid-9091/islam-studie_aid_263343.html (22.08.2008)

MEEL, P. E. (1954): *Clinical versus Statistical Prediction: A Theoretical Analysis and a Review of the Evidence.* Minneapolis.

MELANDER, I. (2008): *EU eyes air passenger profiling in 2009.* Available at: http://www.reuters.com/article/domesticNews/idUSL2579300020080125 (20.07.2008)

METROPOLITAN POLICE (2008): *MPS Home. Stop and Search FAQ's.* Available at: http://www.met.police.uk/stopandsearch/what_is.htm (20.07.2008)

MOECKLI, D. (2006): *Terrorist Profiling and the Importance of a Proactive Approach to Human Rights Protection.* In: *Annual Conference of the Association of Human Rights Institutes.* Vienna.

MOECKLI, D. (2008): *Human Rights and Non-Discrimination in the ,War on Terror'.* Oxford & New York.

THE MUSLIM COUNCIL OF BRITAIN (2004): *Have Your Say on Police ,Stop and Search' Powers.*
Available at: http://mcb.org.uk/features/features.php?ann_id=500 (15.07.2008)

O'NEILL, S. (2004): *Detained terrorism suspects at highest level since 1970s.*
Available at: http://www.timesonline.co.uk/tol/news/uk/article407101.ece?token=null&offset=0&page=1 (29.07.2008)

NEW SOUTH WALES COUNCIL FOR CIVIL LIBERTIES INC. (2006): *NSW Police settle out of court in wrongful arrest case.*
Available at: http://www.nswccl.org.au/news/show_pr.php?relNum=6&relYear=2006 (20.09.2008)

NEW YORK TIMES (1986): *Jordanian is found guilty; Gets 45 years in El Al plot.*
Available at: http://select.nytimes.com/gst/abstract.html?res=F50714FF3F5A0C768EDDA90994DE484D81 (02.10.2008)

NORFOLK, A. (2007): *The unexpected profile of the modern terrorist: 26, from a caring family, married, with children, graduate.*
Available at: http://www.timesonline.co.uk/tol/news/uk/crime/article2039865.ece (04.09.2008)

NOWAK, P. (2006): *Nur bei konkreter Gefahr.*
Available at: http://www.heise.de/tp/r4/artikel/22/22731/1.html (31.07.2008)

OFFICE OF PUBLIC SECTOR INFORMATION (2000): *Terrorism Act 2000. Chapter 11 Arrangement of Sections. 20 July 2000.*
Available at: http://www.opsi.gov.uk/acts/acts2000/ukpga_20000011_en_5#pt5-pb2-l1g44 (16.07.2008)

OFFICE OF PUBLIC SECTOR INFORMATION (2006): *Terrorism Act 2006. Chapter 11. 30 March 2006.*
Available at: http://www.opsi.gov.uk/acts/acts2006/ukpga_20060011_en_1(09.08.2008)

OPEN SOCIETY JUSTICE INITIATIVE (2007): *Ethnic Profiling in Europe: Counter-Terrorism Activities and the Creation of Suspect Communities.*
Available at: http://www.ecre.org/files/Ethnic%20profiling%20in%20Europe%20English.pdf (22.07.2008)

PATERSON, T. (2005): *Raids on mosques broke terror network, claim German police.*
Available at: http://findarticles.com/p/articles/mi_qn4158/is_20050113/ai_n9694352 (22.07.2008)

PETERS, D. (2007): *Terrorismus: US-Geheimdienste gaben Tipp zur Verhaftung.*
Available at: http://www.berlinkontor.de/08.09.2007/terrorismus-us-geheimdienste-gaben-tipp-zur-verhaftung.html (17.08.2008)

POLICE HOME OFFICE (1984): *Police and Criminal Evidence Act 1984. Code A.*
Available at: http://police.homeoffice.gov.uk/publications/operational-policing/previous-PACE-codes-2005/PACE_Chapter_A.pdf?view=Binary (17.07.2008)

PRIAR, L.L./MARTIN, T.F. (1954): *Searching and Disarming Criminals.* In: *Public Science (1954):* 481.

PRIVACY INTERNATIONAL (2005): *Terrorism Profile - EU.*
Available at: http://www.privacyinternational.org/article.shtml?cmd%5B347%5D=x-347-508362 (02.08.2008)

RASINYA, D. (1999): *The Color Of Suspicion.*
Available at: http://query.nytimes.com/gst/fullpage.html?res=9A06E7DC1E3DF932A25754C0A96F958260 (18.08.2008)

ROSE, K. (2006): *Allianzen aus Sicht globaler Wirtschaftsunternehmen. Zukünftige Entwicklungen und ihre Auswirkungen auf Sicherheitsallianzen.* In: BUNDESKRIMINALAMT, Ed. (2005): *Neue Allianzen gegen Kriminalität und Gewalt. Ganzheitlicher Ansatz zur Kriminalitätsbekämpfung – national und international-. München:* 7-16.

SANDERS, J.: *Walk the Walk: Gait Recognition Technology could identify Humans at a Distance.*
Available at: http://gtresearchnews.gatech.edu/newsrelease/GAIT.htm (21.07.2008)

SCHIFFAUER, W. (2006): *Verfassungsschutz und islamische Gemeinden.* In: U. KEMMESIES, Ed. (2006): *Terrorismus und Extremismus – der Zukunft auf der Spur.* München: 237 – 254.

SCHILY, O.(2005): *Die Bildung von Allianzen gegen Kriminalität und Gewalt als nationale und internationale sicherheitspolitische Herausforderung.* In: BUNDESKRIMINALAMT, Ed. (2005): *Neue Allianzen gegen Kriminalität und Gewalt. Ganzheitlicher Ansatz zur Kriminalitätsbekämpfung – national und international.* München: 7-16.

SECURE COMMUNITY NETWORK (2005): *Seven Signs of Terrorist Activity.*
Available at: http://www.scnus.org/page.aspx?ID=101218 (13.08.2008)

SHAPIRO, J. (2008): *Detention of Terrorism Suspects in Britain and France.*
Available at: http://www.brookings.edu/testimony/2008/0715_terrorism_shapiro.aspx (29.07.2008)

SHERMAN, L.W. (1993): *Defiance, Deterrence, and Irrelevance: A Theory of the Criminal Sanction.* In: *Journal of Research in Crime and Delinquency 30 (4):* 445-473.

SPIEGEL ONLINE (2005): *Briten in Dubai nach Londoner Anschlägen misshandelt.*
Available at: http://www.spiegel.de/panorama/0,1518,368116,00.html (27.08.2008)

STAKELBECK, E. (2007): *Terrorist Profiling and Political Correctness: A Bad Mix.*
Available at: http://www.cbn.com/cbnnews/news/050826b.aspx (13.08.2008)

STATEWATCH (2005): *‚Terrorist' lists – monitoring proscription, designation and asset-freezing.*
Available at: http://www.statewatch.org/terrorlists/terrorlists.html (01.09.2008)

STATEWATCH (2007): *PNR (passenger name record) scheme proposed to place under surveillance all travel in and out of the EU.*
Available at: http://www.statewatch.org/news/2007/nov/01eu-pnr.htm (20.07.2008)

STINSON, J. (2006): *EU discuss anti-terror efforts, balance of liberty and security.*
Available at: http://www.usatoday.com/news/world/2006-08-16-britain-reid_x.htm (20.07.2008)

TALKISLAM (2007): *Re: Q2. Has terrorism act made an impact on your community?*
Available at: http://blog.talkislam.co.uk/blog/_archives/2007/9/27/3256416.html (27.08.2008)

TIGNER, B. (2007): *The pros and cons of EU racial profiling.*
Available at: http://www.speroforum.com/site/article.asp?idCategory=35&idarticle=9773 (22.07.2008)

TOCQUEVILLE, A. DE (1961): *Democracy in America, Vol. II.* New York.

TOMIK, S. (2007): *„Unter dem Deckmantel der Unschuldigen".*
Available at: http://www.faz.net/s/Rub99C3EECA60D84C08AD-6B3E60C4EA807F/Doc~EFB4F08C88E044044B9FF33FC7B807705~ATpl~Ecommon~Scontent.html

TRAVIS, A. (2006a): *Use of ‚stop and search' terror law alienating Muslims, warns Yard.*
Available at: http://www.guardian.co.uk/uk/2006/feb/17/terrorism.politics/print (17.07.2008)

TRAVIS, A. (2006b): *Europe-wide security-net to counter terrorism.* Available at: http://www.guardian.co.uk/politics/2006/aug/17/terrorism.immigrationpolicy (19.07.2008)

UHLMANN, M. (2008): *European Converts to Terrorism.* Available at: http://www.meforum.org/article/1927 (04.09.2008)

UNITED NATIONS (1969): *International Convention on the Elimination of all Forms of Racial Discrimination. 4 January 1969.* Available at: http://www2.ohchr.org/english/law/cerd.htm (05.08.2008)

UNITED NATIONS (1976): *International Covenant on Civil and Political Rights. 23 March 1976.* Available at: http://www2.ohchr.org/english/law/ccpr.htm (06.08.2008)

UNITED NATIONS (1979): *Document A/RES/34/169 "Code of Conduct for Law Enforcement Officials. 17 December 1979".* Available at: http://daccessdds.un.org/doc/RESOLUTION/GEN/NR0/377/96/IMG/NR037796.pdf?OpenElement (09.08.2008)

UNITED NATIONS (2001): *World Conference against Racism, Racial Discrimination, Xenophobia and Related Intolerance. 8. September 2001.* Available at: http://www.unhchr.ch/pdf/Durban.pdf (05.08.2008)

UNITED NATIONS OFFICE OF THE HIGH COMMISSIONER FOR HUMAN RIGHTS (2003): *Digest of Jurisprudence of the UN and Regional Organizations on the Protection of Human Rights While Countering Terrorism.* Available at:http://www.ohchr.org/Documents/Publications/DigestJurisprudenceen.pdf (17.09.2008)

UNWATCHED (2007): *Europäische Kommission will Profile von allen Passagieren innerhalb und außerhalb der EU.* Available at: http://www.unwatched.org/node/720

WALLACE, N. (2005): *Payout for lawyer dragged from court.* Available at: http://www.smh.com.au/news/national/payout-for-lawyer-dragged-from-court/2005/10/25/1130239521799.html (20.09.2008)

WANZECK, M. (2007): *Terror-Festnahmen. Die Verdächtigen und ihre Hintergründe.* Available at: http://www.stern.de/politik/deutschland/597074.html (18.06.2008)

WHITLOCK, C. (2007): *Terrorists Proving Harder to Profile.*
Available at: http://www.washingtonpost.com/wp-dyn/content/article/2007/03/11/AR2007031101618.html (04.09.2008)

WIBERG, H.(1990): *Konflikt teori och fredsforskning. (conflict theory and peace research).* Stockholm.

ZAKARIA, F. (2002): *Delicate Balance: The Case for „Smart Profiling" as a Weapon in the War on Terror.*
Available at: http://fareedzakaria.com/ARTICLES/newsweek/070802_security.html (05.09.2008)

ZALMAN, A. (2008a): *Controversial Counterterrorism and Security Technologies. Radio Frequency ID.*
Available at: http://terrorism.about.com/od/controversialtechnologies/g/RFIDs.htm (20.07.2008)

ZALMAN, A. (2008b): *Biometric identifications are only as fair and objective as the political intentions behind them.*
Available at: http://terrorism.about.com/od/controversialtechnologies/i/Biometrics_2.htm (20.07.2008)

ZALMAN, A. (2008c): *Artificial Intelligence (AI).*
Available at: http://terrorism.about.com/od/controversialtechnologies/g/ArtificialIntel.htm (30.07.2008)

ZALMAN, A. (2008d): *Genetic Algorithms.*
Available at: http://terrorism.about.com/od/g/g/GeneticAlgorith.htm (30.07.2008)

ZALMAN, A. (2008e):*What is Data Mining and What Does it Have to Do with Counterterrorism.*
Available at: http://terrorism.about.com/od/counterterrorism/a/DataMining.htm?p=1 (30.07.2008)

ZALMAN, A. (2008f): *Terrorist Groups – A list of Terrorist Groups by Type.*
Available at: http://terrorism.about.com/od/groupsleader1/a/TerroristGroups.htm (08.08.2008)

Hamburger Studien zur Kriminologie und Kriminalpolitik
hrsg. von Prof. Dr. Susanne Krasmann. Prof. Dr. Fritz Sack, Prof. Dr. Sebastian Scheerer, Prof. Dr. Klaus Sessar, Prof. Dr. Bernhard Villmow und Prof. Dr. Peter Wetzels

Stephan Heinrich
Innere Sicherheit und neue Informations- und Kommunikationstechnologien
Veränderungen des Politikfeldes zwischen institutionellen Faktoren, Akteursorientierung und technologischen Entwicklungen
Die Technisierung der Polizeien steht im Spannungsfeld zwischen der Utopie verbesserter Kriminalitätsbekämpfung und -verminderung sowie entgegengesetzt dem Bedrohungsbild allmächtiger Sicherheitsorganisationen. Die dabei ablaufenden Prozesse und ihre Akteure ebenso wie der Einfluss kriminalpolitischer Programme wurden bislang nur lückenhaft dokumentiert und untersucht. Mit neuen technischen Potenzialen führt die Informatisierung zur Entstehung eines umfassenden sozio-technischen Sicherheitssystems, das sich zunehmend der Steuerung und Kontrolle durch verwaltungsexterne und -interne Akteure entzieht.
Bd. 42, 2007, 496 S., 34,90 €, br., ISBN 978-3-8258-0430-5